Deep Learning in Gaming and Animations

Explainable AI (XAI) for Engineering Applications
Series Editors: Aditya Khamparia and Deepak Gupta

Explainable AI (XAI) has developed as a subfield of artificial intelligence, focusing on exposing complex AI models to humans in a systematic and interpretable manner. This area explores, discusses the steps and models involved in making intelligent decisions. This series will cover the working behavior and explains the ability of powerful algorithms such as neural networks, ensemble methods including random forests, and other similar algorithms to sacrifice transparency and explainability for power, performance, and accuracy in different engineering applications relates to the real world. Aimed at graduate students, academic researchers, and professionals, the proposed series will focus key topics including XAI techniques for engineering applications, Explainable AI for deep neural network predictions, XAI for machine learning predictions, XAI-driven recommendation systems for automobile and manufacturing industries, and XAI for autonomous vehicles.

Deep Learning in Gaming and Animations: Principles and Applications
Vikas Chaudhary, Moolchand Sharma, Prerna Sharma, and Deevyankar Agarwal

For more information about this series, please visit: https://www.routledge.com/Explainable-AI-XAI-for-Engineering-Applications/book-series/CRCEAIFEA

Deep Learning in Gaming and Animations

Principles and Applications

Edited by

Vikas Chaudhary, Moolchand Sharma, Prerna Sharma, and Deevyankar Agarwal

CRC Press
Taylor & Francis Group
Boca Raton London New York

CRC Press is an imprint of the
Taylor & Francis Group, an **informa** business

First edition published 2022
by CRC Press
6000 Broken Sound Parkway NW, Suite 300, Boca Raton, FL 33487-2742

and by CRC Press
2 Park Square, Milton Park, Abingdon, Oxon, OX14 4RN

First edition published by CRC Press 2022

CRC Press is an imprint of Taylor & Francis Group, LLC

Library of Congress Cataloging-in-Publication Data

Names: Chaudhary, Vikas, editor. | Sharma, Moolchand, editor. | Sharma, Prerna, editor. | Agarwal, Deevyankar, editor.
Title: Deep learning in gaming and animations : principles and applications / edited by Vikas Chaudhary, Moolchand Sharma, Prerna Sharma and Deevyankar Agarwal.
Description: Boca Raton : CRC Press, 2022. | Series: Explainable ai (xai) for engineering applications | Includes bibliographical references and index.
Identifiers: LCCN 2021030248 (print) | LCCN 2021030249 (ebook) | ISBN 9781032126098 (hardback) | ISBN 9781003231530 (ebook)
Subjects: LCSH: Object-oriented programming (Computer science) | Artificial intelligence.
Classification: LCC QA76.64 .D437 2022 (print) | LCC QA76.64 (ebook) | DDC 005.1/17–dc23
LC record available at https://lccn.loc.gov/2021030248
LC ebook record available at https://lccn.loc.gov/2021030249

ISBN: 9781032126098 (hbk)
ISBN: 9781032139302 (pbk)
ISBN: 9781003231530 (ebk)

DOI: 10.1201/9781003231530

Typeset in Times LT Std
by KnowledgeWorks Global Ltd.

Dedication

Dr. Vikas Chaudhary would like to dedicate this book to his father Sh. Rajendra Singh and his mother Smt. Santosh for their constant support and motivation; and his family members, including his wife Ms. Amita Panwar, his daughter Astha Chaudhary, and his sons Shivansh Chaudhary and Anmol Chaudhary. I would also like to give my special thanks to the publisher and my other co-editors for having faith in my abilities. Before all and after all, the main thanks should be to the Almighty God.

Mr. Moolchand Sharma would like to dedicate this book to his father Sh. Naresh Kumar Sharma and his mother Smt. Rambati Sharma, for their constant support and motivation, and his family members, including his wife Ms. Pratibha Sharma and his son Dhairya Sharma. I would also like to give my special thanks to the publisher and my other co-editors for having faith in my abilities.

Ms. Prerna Sharma would like to dedicate this book to her father Mr. Vipin Sharma, mother Ms. Suman Sharma, husband Mr. Parminder Mann and her family for their support and constant motivation. Specially dedicated to her beloved sons Pratyaksh, Kairav & Kevin Mann

Mr. Deevyankar Agarwal would like to dedicate this book to his father Sh. Anil Kumar Agarwal and his mother Smt. Sunita Agarwal, and his wife Ms. Aparna Agarwal, and his son Jai Agarwal for their constant support and motivation. I would also like to give my special thanks to the publisher and my other co-editors for having faith in my abilities.

Contents

List of Figures and Tables..ix

Preface.. xiii

Editors... xv

Contributors xvii

Chapter 1   Checkers-AI 1

Priyanshi Gupta, Vividha and Preeti Nagrath

Chapter 2   The Future of Automatically Generated Animation with AI............. 19

Preety Khatri

Chapter 3   Artificial Intelligence as Futuristic Approach for Narrative Gaming.... 37

Toka Haroun, Vikas Rao Naidu, and Aparna Agarwal

Chapter 4   Review on Using Artificial Intelligence Related Deep Learning
Techniques in Gaming and Recent Networks 65

*Mujahid Tabassum, Sundresan Perumal, Hadi Nabipour
Afrouzi, Saad Bin Abdul Kashem, and Waqar Hassan*

Chapter 5   A Review on Deep Learning Algorithms for Image Processing
in Gaming and Animations.. 91

*Sugandha Chakraverti, Ashish Kumar Chakraverti, Piyush
Bhushan Singh, and Rakesh Ranjan*

Chapter 6   Artificial Intelligence in Games.. 103

Abhisht Joshi, Moolchand Sharma, and Jafar Al Zubi

Chapter 7   A Framework for Estimation of Generative Models Through
an Adversarial Process for Production of Animated Gaming
Characters... 123

Saad Bin Khalid and Bramah Hazela

Chapter 8   Generative Adversarial Networks Based PCG for Games............... 137

Nimisha Mittal, Priyanjali Pratap Singh, and Prerna Sharma

Index... 157

List of Figures and Tables

FIGURES

Figure 1.1   An example of payoff matrix for a zero-sum two-player game..........4

Figure 1.2   Code implementation of the heuristic function. 5

Figure 1.3   Binary Search tree example...6

Figure 1.4   A Minimax tree 7

Figure 1.5   Algorithmic representation of a Minimax tree example. 7

Figure 1.6   Alpha-Beta pruning illustration..8

Figure 1.7   Alpha-Beta pruning illustration..9

Figure 1.8   Alpha-Beta pruning illustration..10

Figure 1.9   Flowchart depicting the implementation algorithm. 11

Figure 1.10   Before single capture of a piece..12

Figure 1.11   After single capture of a piece...13

Figure 1.12   Before multiple capture of pieces 13

Figure 1.13   After multiple capture of pieces 13

Figure 1.14   Upgradation of a piece into king on reaching the end side of
the opponent...14

Figure 1.15   Displaying the result of the game 14

Figure 1.16   Use case flowchart 15

Figure 1.17   System environment diagram 16

Figure 2.1   Setting up keyframes for timing the bouncing balls. 20

Figure 2.2   Classification of autonomous agents...22

Figure 2.3   A topology of agent 23

Figure 2.4   Five emerging technologies that will change the world in next
five years. 26

Figure 2.5   Attractive opportunities in the 3D animation market......................34

Figure 3.1   The MDA framework 49

Figure 3.2   Proposed functionality diagram 52

Figure 3.3 Player character class in UE4 53

Figure 3.4 First person game view 53

Figure 3.5 Inspect item prompt 54

Figure 3.6 Player picks item 54

Figure 3.7 Item inspection 55

Figure 3.8 User interface 55

Figure 3.9 Main menu 56

Figure 3.10 Journal blueprint 56

Figure 3.11 Player hunger and stamina 57

Figure 3.12 Blueprint of AI based functionality 57

Figure 3.13 Overview of the scene 58

Figure 3.14 User interface of game design platform – Unreal Engine. 59

Figure 3.15 AI behavior tree for the two stages of Q-learning. 61

Figure 4.1 Difference of M2M and IoT 70

Figure 4.2 Bluetooth Communication 71

Figure 4.3 IoT operating layer model 73

Figure 4.4 Top 10 IoT involved industries 73

Figure 4.5 IoT application and industries 76

Figure 4.6 First order model framework 77

Figure 4.7 Wireless network growth 79

Figure 4.8 Overview of AI 80

Figure 4.9 Machine learning algorithm 81

Figure 4.10 Decision tree example 82

Figure 4.11 Data Analytics 85

Figure 5.1 Computer "vision" via data. 96

Figure 5.2 Classification of object detection, here, the self-driving car. 96

Figure 5.3 Examples of different transfer functions applied to an image:
(a) original, (b) logarithmic, (c) histogram equalization, and
(d) negative 98

Figure 6.1 Comparison of gaming industry size with other industries 105

Figure 6.2 Making AI model to adapt the physics laws 109

Figure 6.3 Unique experience of VR 109

Figure 6.4 AR used in Pokémon Go 110

Figure 6.5 AR vs. VR 110

Figure 6.6 Extend reality with AR, MR, and VR 111

Figure 6.7 Evolution of game characters 111

Figure 6.8 Evolution of graphics in Need for Speed 112

Figure 6.9 Reinforcement learning 113

Figure 6.10 AlphaGo Zero beating Ke Jei 113

Figure 6.11 Minimax tree for Tic-Tac-Toe 116

Figure 6.12 The finite state machine for a real time strategy worker NPC 117

Figure 6.13 Implementation of an A* graph to find the best way. 117

Figure 6.14 Dota 2 hero AI for long-horizon learning 119

Figure 7.1 Graph of loss of Generator and Discriminator in CGAN 135

Figure 8.1 Evolution of GAN in video games 143

TABLES

Table 2.1 Agent Properties Based on the Coordination, Planning, and
Cooperative Ability 24

Table 2.2 Summary of AR Frameworks 28

Table 2.3 A Summary of Game Engines 29

Table 3.1 Levels of Fear (See Ntokos, 2018) 47

Table 4.1 Overview of ML Algorithm used in IoT Networks 83

Table 4.2 Overview of IoT Applications, Protocols and Algorithm 86

Table 8.1 Main Contributions of the Above Explored Algorithms 147

Table 8.2 Popular Datasets in Video Game Content Generation 150

Preface

We are delighted to launch our book, "Deep Learning in Gaming and Animations: Principles and Applications." Artificial intelligence has been a growing resource for video games for years now. Most video games—whether they are racing games, shooting games, or strategy games—have various elements controlled by AI, such as the enemy bots or neutral characters. Even the ambiguous characters that do not seem to be doing much are programmed to add more depth to the game and give you clues about your next steps. Today's modern world is currently under a significant influence on innovative technologies such as artificial intelligence, deep learning, machine learning, and IoT. This book aims to present the various approaches, techniques, and applications that are available in the field of gaming and animations. It is a valuable source of knowledge for researchers, engineers, practitioners, and graduate and doctoral students working in the same field. It will also be helpful for faculty members of graduate schools and universities. Around 25 full-length chapters were received. Amongst these manuscripts, eight chapters have been included in this volume. All the chapters submitted were peer-reviewed by at least two independent reviewers, provided with a detailed review proforma. The comments from the reviewers were communicated to the authors, who incorporated the suggestions in their revised manuscripts. The recommendations from two reviewers were taken into consideration while selecting chapters for inclusion in this volume. The exhaustiveness of the review process is evident, given the large number of articles received addressing a wide range of research areas. The stringent review process ensured that each published chapter met the rigorous academic and scientific standards.

We would also like to thank the authors of the published chapters for adhering to the schedule and incorporating the review comments. We wish to extend my heartfelt acknowledgment to the authors, peer-reviewers, committee members, and production staff whose diligent work shaped this volume. We especially want to thank our dedicated team of peer-reviewers who volunteered for the arduous and tedious step of quality checking and critique on the submitted chapters.

Vikas Chaudhary,
Moolchand Sharma,
Prerna Sharma,
Deevyankar Agarwal,
Editors,
October 5, 2021

Editors

Vikas Chaudhary is a professor in the Computer Science & Engineering department at JIMS Engineering Management Technical Campus, Greater Noida. He has 18 years of teaching and research experience. He obtained a Doctorate from the National Institute of Technology, Kurukshetra, India, in Machine Learning/Unsupervised Learning. He has published various research papers in the International Journals of Springer, Elsevier, Taylor & Francis. Also, he has published various papers in IEEE International Conferences and national conferences. He is a reviewer of Springer Journal as well as of many IEEE conferences. He has written a book on Cryptography & Network Security. His research area is machine learning, artificial neural networks.

Moolchand Sharma is an Assistant Professor in the Department of Computer Science and Engineering at Maharaja Agrasen Institute of Technology, GGSIPU Delhi. He has published scientific research publications in reputed International Journals and Conferences, including SCI indexed and Scopus indexed Journals such as Cognitive Systems Research (Elsevier), Physical Communication(Elsevier), Intelligent Decision Technologies: An International Journal, Cyber-Physical Systems (Taylor & Francis Group), International Journal of Image & Graphics (World Scientific), International Journal of Innovative Computing and Applications (Inderscience) & Innovative Computing and Communication Journal (Scientific Peer-reviewed Journal). He has authored/co-authored chapters with such international publishers as Elsevier, Wiley, and De Gruyter. He has authored/edited three books with CRC Press and Bhavya Books. His research area includes artificial intelligence, nature-inspired computing, security in cloud computing, machine learning, and search engine optimization. He is associated with various professional bodies like ISTE, IAENG, ICSES, UACEE, Internet Society, etc. He possesses teaching experience of more than nine years. He is the co-convener of the ICICC-2018, ICICC-2019& ICICC-2020 springer conference series and also the co-convener of ICCRDA-2020 Scopus Indexed IOP Material Science & Engineering conference series. He is also the reviewer of many reputed journals like Springer, Elsevier, IEEE, Wiley, Taylor & Francis Group and World Scientific Journal, and many springer conferences. He is currently a doctoral researcher at DCR University of Science & Technology, Haryana. He completed his Post Graduate in 2012 from SRM University, NCR Campus, Ghaziabad and graduated in 2010 from KNGD Modi Engg. College, GBTU.

Prerna Sharma is an Assistant Professor in the Department of Computer Science and Engineering at Maharaja Agrasen Institute of Technology, GGSIPU Delhi. She has authored/co-authored SCI-indexed journal and Scopus indexed journal articles in high ranked and prestigious journals such as Journal of Supercomputing (Springer), Cognitive Systems Research(Elsevier), Expert Systems (Wiley) International Journal of Innovative Computing and Applications (Inderscience). She has also authored book chapters with International level publishers (Wiley and Elsevier). She has extensively worked on Computational Intelligence. Her area of interest includes artificial intelligence, machine learning, nature-inspired computing, soft computing, and cloud computing. She is associated with various professional bodies like IAENG, ICSES, UACEE, Internet Society, etc. She has a rich academic background and teaching experience of 8 years. She is a doctoral researcher at Delhi Technological University (DTU), Delhi. She completed her Post Graduate in 2011 from USIT, GGSIPU, and Graduate in 2009 from GPMCE, GGSIPU.

Deevyankar Agarwal works as a lecturer in the Engineering Department–EEE Section (Computer Engineering) at the University of Technology & Applied Sciences (Public University), Muscat, Oman. He has 20 years of teaching and research experience. He is currently a doctoral researcher at the University of Valladolid, Spain. He has published various research papers in the International Journals of Springer, Elsevier, Taylor & Francis. Also, he has published various papers in IEEE International Conferences and national conferences. He is a reviewer for Springer Journals as well as of many IEEE conferences. He is a Doctoral researcher from University of Valladolid, Spain. He completed his M.TECH (Computer Science & Eng.) in 2008 from GGSIP University, M.Sc (Computer Science) in 2001 from Agra University (State University), Agra & B.Sc (Computer Science) in 1998 M.J.P Rohilkhand University (State University), Bareilly.

Contributors

Hadi Nabipour Afrouzi
Faculty of Engineering, Computing and
    Science,
Swinburne University of Technology,
Sarawak, Malaysia

Aparna Agarwal
Department of Engineering,
Middle East College (OMAN),
Muscat

Jafar Al Zubi
Computer Engineering department,
Al-Balqa Applied University, School of
    Engineering,
Jordan

Ashish Kumar Chakraverti
Department of Computer Science and
    Engineering,
PSIT College of Engineering,
Kanpur UP, India

Sugandha Chakraverti
Department of Computer Science and
    Engineering,
PSIT College of Engineering,
Kanpur UP, India

Priyanshi Gupta
Department of Computer Science and
    Engineering Department,
Bharati Vidyapeeth's College of
    Engineering,
New Delhi

Toka Haroun
Department of Computing, Department
    of Engineering,
Middle East College (OMAN)

Waqar Hassan
Research and Finance,
Barani Institute of Sciences, Pakistan &
    JV Arid Agriculture University,
Pakistan

Bramah Hazela
Amity School of Engineering &
    Technology Lucknow,
Amity University,
Uttar Pradesh, India

Abhisht Joshi
Department of Information Technology,
    MAIT,
Delhi, India

Saad Bin Abdul Kashem
Qatar Armed Forces – Academic
    Bridge Program,
Qatar Foundation,
Qatar

Saad Bin Khalid
Amity School of Engineering &
    Technology Lucknow,
Amity University,
Uttar Pradesh, India

Preety Khatri
Information Technology,
Institute of Management Studies,
Noida, India

Preeti Nagrath
Department of Computer Science and
    Engineering Department,
Bharati Vidyapeeth's College of
    Engineering,
New Delhi

Vikas Rao Naidu
Department of Engineering,
Middle East College (OMAN),
Muscat

Nimisha Mittalella
Department of Computer Science &
    Engineering,
Maharaja Agrasen Institute of
    Technology,
New Delhi, India

Sundresan Perumal
Faculty of Science and Technology,
Universiti Sains Islam,
Malaysia

Rakesh Ranjan
Department of Computer Science and
    Engineering,
PSIT College of Engineering,
Kanpur UP, India

Moolchand Sharma
Department of Computer Science &
    Engineering,
Maharaja Agrasen Institute of
    Technology,
New Delhi, India

Prerna Sharma
Department of Computer Science &
    Engineering,
Maharaja Agrasen Institute of
    Technology,
New Delhi, India

Piyush Bhushan Singh
Department of Computer Science and
    Engineering,
PSIT College of Engineering,
Kanpur UP, India

Priyanjali Pratap Singh
Department of Computer Science &
    Engineering,
Maharaja Agrasen Institute of
    Technology,
New Delhi, India

Mujahid Tabassum
Faculty of Science and Technology,
Universiti Sains Islam,
Malaysia

Vividha
Department of Computer Science and
    Engineering Department,
Bharati Vidyapeeth's College of
    Engineering,
New Delhi

1 Checkers-AI

American Checkers Game Using Game Theory and Artificial Intelligence Algorithms

Priyanshi Gupta, Vividha and Preeti Nagrath

CONTENTS

1.1 Introduction 1
1.2 Related Work 2
1.3 Methodology 3
    1.3.1 Game Theory 3
    1.3.2 Zero-Sum Game 3
    1.3.3 Heuristic Function 4
    1.3.4 Search Tree 6
    1.3.5 Minimax Approach 6
    1.3.6 Alpha-Beta Pruning 8
    1.3.7 Minimax vs Alpha-Beta Pruning 8
1.4 Implementation 9
    1.4.1 Game Algorithm 9
    1.4.2 Graphical User Interface 12
1.5 Utility and Application 14
    1.5.1 System Environment 15
1.6 Conclusion and Future Scope 16
    1.6.1 Conclusion 16
    1.6.2 Future Scope 16
References 17

1.1 INTRODUCTION

For years, the application of artificial intelligence (AI) in video games has been growing steadily. The bulk of video games have multiple controllable traits, such as racing games, fighting games, etc. [1]. AI is one of the computer sciences fields that can be used to construct a variety of intelligent games, whether board games, video

DOI: 10.1201/9781003231530-1

games, or educational games, that would respond to a human being and that a computer machine would not be able to react to them [2].

The suggested game checkers are one of the most played board games that involve thought and tactics to win the game, or if it was not played properly and used the methods that would allow the player to win, it would be easy to lose. Checkers is a series of two-player strategy board games that include diagonal movements of game pieces [3]. *American checkers* are the most common form of checker. In the popular "checkerboard" pattern, with 12 parts per hand, it is played on an 8 × 8 board of light and dark squares. It is played by two players, as with all types of checkers, taking turns on opposite sides of the board. Black, red, or white are the typical pieces. By hopping over them, enemy bits are captured. The interactions between the pieces are very less in checkers as compared to chess due to different types of pieces. In AI, the heuristic solution definition is based on awareness or study of the reasoning of people. In order to solve a problem, a heuristic approach is faster than traditional methods. The goal of the heuristic is to find a solution that is adequate within a suitable amount of time to solve the problem. A way of evaluating the quest for the target is the heuristic approach. This chapter is divided into several sections. The first section gives an introduction of checkers games and its probable computations along with rules. The second section is the literature survey which tells about the existing computer programs to solve checkers and its history associated with it. The third section is the methodology section which gives details about the methods and fields used in the project. The fourth section is the implementation section in which the applicative view of the algorithm is briefly explained along with implementation of graphical user interface (GUI) in the game and its snapshots. The fifth section is the utility and application section which tells the basic uses, features, and the system environment of the game developed. The last section is the conclusion section in which results and findings along with future scope of the project is mentioned.

1.2 RELATED WORK

Christopher Strachey developed the first computer software for the *American checkers* in February 1951, at the National Physical Laboratory (NPL) in London [4].

It ran on NPLs Pilot Automatic Computing Engine (Pilot ACE) for the first time on 30 July 1951. IBM researcher Arthur Samuel wrote the second machine program in 1956. In the research process, we discovered that a search tree of board positions which can be viewed from the current state was the key feature of the software. Samuel applied Alpha-Beta pruning [5], although he had only a very small amount of machine memory available. A score mechanism was established at any given time, depending on the location of the board, instead of looking for each direction before it came to the end of the game. On each hand, this feature tried to determine the probability of winning on every turn. Many factors were taken into consideration such as the number of pieces each player has or the number of kings and the position of the pieces to the kings were taken into consideration. The program chose its move based on the Minimax method [6]. In 1989, a team at the University of Alberta headed by Jonathan Schaeffer published the most powerful software named Chinook. It was the first computer machine to win the title of world champion in the game for checkers against a human. The Chinook software program contains an opening book, an archive for starting moves from games played by grandmasters with a deep search algorithm which is an efficient motion evaluation feature; and an eight or less piece end-game database for all positions. Because many previous inventions in the gaming industry have been done using the search tree and heuristic function technique, we chose to use Alpha-Beta pruning algorithm as a major emphasis for this article. Different search algorithms were developed before the Alpha-Beta pruning aimed to minimize the tree search. In other games, such as chess, checkers, tic-tac-toe, Isola, and many more, this algorithm has been used.

1.3 METHODOLOGY

The different techniques studied and discussed to understand and implement the checkers game are as follows.

1.3.1 GAME THEORY

While checkers game is a "solved game," which means a computer has to be programmed in a way that will never lose a game. The method of decision-making has to involve decision-makers, actors, environmental variables, priorities, policies, and parameters. The efficiency of the decision-making process in competitive markets relies on assessing all environmental considerations and analyzing them according to objectives. The aim of policy makers is to identify optimum solutions for competing priorities. Game theory is a mathematics-based methodology in which player tactics are reciprocally tested by considering environmental effects [7]. Games theory provides methods for analyzing situations in which interdependent decisions are taken by individuals, called players. This interdependence enables both players to predict the other player's possible choice and strategies to formulate one's strategic move. As a solution to a game, player's preferences and the outcomes that may result from these choices are represented. The science of games has been extended to a wide range of circumstances in which players' decisions interfere to influence the result. The theory both supplements and goes beyond the classical theory of probability in emphasizing the strategic dimensions of decision-making, or aspects regulated by the players rather than by pure chance.

1.3.2 ZERO-SUM GAME

A *zero-sum* game is a mathematical definition of a circumstance in which the benefit or loss in profit of each player is exactly accounted for by the losses or gains in utility of the other players in game theory. The key difference between a general game and a zero-sum game is that the agents have opposite utilities in a *zero-sum* game as opposed to the independent utilities in a general game or a non-zero-sum game. If the participants' net gains are added and the combined losses are subtracted, they will add up to zero. Non-zero-sum, on the other hand, describes a situation where the

Blue / Red	A	B	C
1	30 / - 30	10 / - 10	-20 / 20
2	10 / --10	- 20 / 20	20 / - 20

FIGURE 1.1 An example of payoff matrix for a zero-sum two-player game.

net gains and losses of the involved parties can be less than or greater than zero. A zero-sum game is sometimes called a purely competitive game, whereas non-zero-sum games can be competitive or non-competitive. *Zero-sum* games are most commonly solved using the Minimax theorem, which is directly connected to the duality of linear programming [7], or Nash equilibrium. Many persons have a cognitive predisposition, known as *zero-sum* tendency, to see circumstances as *zero-sum*. The easy representation for a match is a payout matrix. Then the choices are disclosed and the total points of each player are influenced according to the payout for those choices. Consider the two-player *zero-sum* game illustrated in Figure 1.1. The order of play is as follows: one of two secret acts, 1 or 2, is chosen by the first player (red); one of three secret deeds, A, B, or C, is selected by the second player (blue), unaware of the first player's decision. Red will choose Action 2 and Blue will choose Action 1. Red wins 20 points by allocating prizes, while Blue loses 20 points. Rather than agreeing on a single action to be taken, the two players allocate probabilities to their respective actions, and use a random process that selects an action for them according to these probabilities.

Each player tests the odds in order to decrease the estimated overall point loss, regardless of the approach of the opponent. This leads to a linear problem of programming with each player's best solutions. For all *zero-sum* games with two teams, this Minimax approach will possibly determine optimal strategies. The final chance of Red preferring Action 1 is 4/7, and it turned out to be 3/7 for Action 2. For Blue, the odds are 0, 4/7, and 3/7 respectively for acts A, B, and C. Red is the winner with an average of 20/7 points per session.

1.3.3 HEURISTIC FUNCTION

Heuristic, AI, and mathematical optimization in computer science is a concept intended to solve a problem faster when the classical search is too long. For optimality, completeness, accuracy, or speed accuracy, this is done by trading. This could be named, in a way, a shortcut. A heuristic function is a function that, at each branching step, ranks alternatives in search algorithms based on the available knowledge to decide which branch to pursue, through which, the exact solution [8] may be approximated. There is a different sense of heuristic functions used in single-agent search; they return an approximation of the distance of a given state from a target. The heuristic function in this project is used to make the search in the algorithm easier. The heuristic, like the full-space search algorithm, initially tries all possibilities at each point. However, if the present probability is potentially worse than the better alternative discovered, the search can be stopped at any moment. For the heuristic function proposed in this chapter, we theorize that the perfect weight for the king piece can be found, but assigning the king a weight much greater than a standard chip will make the player give the king too much priority, leading to situations where the player potentially damages their odds of winning by losing a king's regular chips. Thus, we have created a balance between the value of a pawn and the value of the king by creating a function called PieceSumDifference.

$$\text{Pawn's Value} = 1$$

$$\text{King's Value} = 3$$

As we can see in Figure 1.2, the function is described and the number of kings and pawns each player has in the current scenario is calculated in order to assign a value and evaluate the position at which the current player is standing.

```
function evaluatePosition(bf)
{

    let rPieceSum = 0;
    let yPieceSum = 0;

    for(let p of bf.rPieces){
        if(bf.board[p] == PIECE_TYPE.SUPER_RED)
        {
            rPieceSum += 3;
        }else if(bf.board[p] == PLAYER.P1){
            rPieceSum++;
        }
    }

    for(let p of bf.yPieces){
        if(bf.board[p] == PIECE_TYPE.SUPER_YELLOW)
        {
            yPieceSum += 3;
        }else if(bf.board[p] == PLAYER.P2){
            yPieceSum++;
        }
    }

    let eval = rPieceSum - yPieceSum;
    return [null, eval];

}
```

FIGURE 1.2 Code implementation of the heuristic function.

The player that maximizes is the red player and the player that minimizes is the yellow player. Therefore, the heuristic value returned is the difference between the values of the player maximizing and the player minimizing.

1.3.4 Search Tree

A search tree is a type of tree data structure which is used within a set to locate specific keys. In order for a search tree to work, the key must be greater for each node than any subtree key on the left and smaller than any subtree key on the right [9]. The key idea is to simulate, using self-play, several thousands of random games from the present place. In a search tree, new positions are added and each tree node includes a value that predicts who is going to win from that position. There are many search-tree data structures, some of which often allow elements to be easily added and removed, and operations must then retain the balance of the tree. The Binary Search tree depicted in Figure 1.3 is implemented in this project.

The Binary Search tree is a node-based binary tree data structure in which every left child is smaller than node and right child is greater than the node.

1.3.5 Minimax Approach

In AI and game theory, Minimax is a decision rule used to minimize the future loss while optimizing the expected advantage. Before applying this strategy, the two assumptions made for the game are the fact that the human player plays optimally and tries to win. The other is that the game should be a game that is purely strategic. The Minimax algorithm is the modified version of the backward-induction algorithm. It can also be considered to maximize the minimum gain called maximin. In two cases, players make simultaneous moves and opposite moves, each player minimizing the other player's overall potential gain. A player therefore maximizes his own minimum advantage, becoming a *zero-sum* game. Minimax and Maximin, however, are not identical. In non-zero-sum game conditions, Maximin can be used.

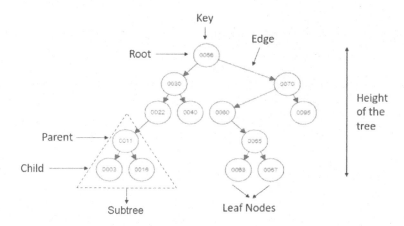

FIGURE 1.3 Binary Search tree example.

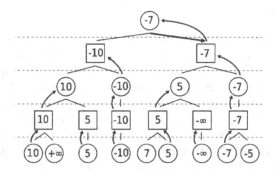

FIGURE 1.4 A Minimax tree.

In this project, the Minimax [10] algorithm is used as a recursive algorithm to determine the moves made by the two players, usually black and white. The two players are competing strategically and usually they have the complete information about the game. In checkers game, there is an integer line and a number line, and any integer which is positive favors white, and any integer which is negative, favors black. So positive infinity would be a win for white and negative infinity would be a loss for black. There is a value assigned to every position of the game which is measured by the heuristic feature defined. The players make moves to maximize the minimum position value based on the assumption that the opponent will follow the predicted moves. If it's white's turn to pass, white provides each of their legal moves with a value. The algorithm conducts what we in computer science call a "depth-first search," as shown in Figure 1.4.

This means that it explores the whole length of the tree vertically, until it reaches the terminal node and then works its way back up. Secondarily, or among other sibling nodes, the algorithm moves horizontally. This is in contrast to a "breadth-first search," which does exactly the reverse. It mostly passes between fellow sibling nodes horizontally, scans at a time for a whole "level," and makes its way down the tree secondarily. The algorithmic representation is shown in Figure 1.5 [11].

```
function minimax(node, depth, maximizingPlayer) is
    if depth = 0 or node is a terminal node then
        return the heuristic value of node
    if maximizingPlayer then
        value := -∞
        for each child of node do
            value := max(value, minimax(child, depth - 1, FALSE))
        return value
    else (* minimizing player *)
        value := +∞
        for each child of node do
            value := min(value, minimax(child, depth - 1, TRUE))
        return value
```

FIGURE 1.5 Algorithmic representation of a Minimax tree example.

1.3.6 ALPHA-BETA PRUNING

Minimax approach amounts to exhaustive search of solution space. In a realistic game such as checkers, the search space is large. It is therefore more efficient to heuristically reduce the search space in case of Minimax solutions. Alpha-Beta pruning algorithm provides a mechanism to decrease the number of counts of the nodes thus reducing the search space in the Minimax tree [12]. Apart from checkers, it is also used in other two-player games. Further, the search is stopped once it encounters a branch where at least a single value has been found that confirms that the branch would be worse in comparison to earlier payoffs. Therefore, these moves can be avoided in the game to reduce unnecessary computation. Alpha-Beta pruning does the same. It discards the branches of the search tree without affecting any of the decisions to return the same result in spite of pruning [13]. Apart from reducing the search time, it is possible to have a deeper search allowing a greater depth of subtree to be scanned. Two values are used in the algorithm, Alpha and Beta. The highest (lowest) score that the optimizing player has is stored in the Alpha variable. Beta value keeps the full score that the player who minimizes is guaranteed to win. The original Alpha value shall be equal to −infinity and Beta value is equal to +infinity. This gap gets smaller as the search continues. When the Beta value gets smaller than the Alpha value, it means that it is possible to limit the search beyond the current node.

In Figure 1.6, Alpha-Beta pruning cuts the gray subtrees while moving from left to right and it is not appropriate to investigate them at every step since the category of subtrees yields the value as a whole of an equal subtree or worse leaving the end result unaffected. The implementation of this algorithm is demonstrated as shown in Figures 1.7 and 1.8.

1.3.7 MINIMAX VS ALPHA-BETA PRUNING

As we know, the Minimax algorithm works with a game tree where the two agents are Max and Min. Max tries to maximize the gain of the game and Min tries to minimize the loss of the game. They are mutually recursive, i.e., Max calls Min, and Min calls Max, and this process takes place all the way to the bottom of the search tree. The Alpha-Beta pruning is introduced as an opportunity to remove branches of the search tree [14], thus, shortening the time to find the "most promising" subtree,

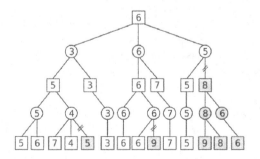

FIGURE 1.6 Alpha-Beta pruning illustration.

```
function minmax(bf, depth, alpha, beta, turn){
    if (depth <= 0 || bf.availableMoves <= 0) return evaluatePosition(bf);
    if(turn == AI){
        let bestScore = -Infinity;
        let bestMove = null;
        let tempBf = tempBfClone(bf);
        for(let pieceMove of tempBf.availableMoves){
            let moves;
            let isCapture = false;

            if(pieceMove.moves.length > 0){
                moves = pieceMove.moves;
            }else{
                moves = pieceMove.captures;
                isCapture = true;
            }
            for(let move of moves){
                createNewNode(tempBf, pieceMove.piece, move, isCapture);
                let value = minmax(tempBf, depth-1, alpha, beta, tempBf.move)[1];
                if (value > bestScore){
                    bestScore = value;
                    bestMove = {src: pieceMove.piece, target: move, capture: isCapture};
                }
                alpha = Math.max(alpha, value);
                tempBf = tempBfClone(bf);
                if(alpha >= beta) break;
            }
            if(alpha >= beta) break;
        }
        return [bestMove, bestScore];
```

FIGURE 1.7 Alpha-Beta pruning illustration.

and allowing a greater search to be done at the same time [15]. It is a member of the algorithm branch and binding class, unlike its predecessor.

Usually, the subtrees are temporarily dominated by either a first player advantage during Alpha-Beta pruning in the case when many first player movements are good, but all second player moves are calculated in order to find a comeback, or vice versa. If the ordering of the move is incorrect, this gain will repeatedly switch sides during the search, it will lead to inefficiency each time. Any step closer to the current position decreases exponentially with the number of searched positions, significant effort is worth focusing on sorting early moves.

1.4 IMPLEMENTATION

The algorithmic implementation and the GUI are described in the following sections.

1.4.1 GAME ALGORITHM

The game algorithm is implemented using JavaScript. Figure 1.9 describes the implementation in the form of a flowchart. The procedure is as the player completes

```
    }else{
        let bestScore = Infinity;
        let bestMove = null;
        let tempBf = tempBfClone(bf);

        for(let pieceMove of tempBf.availableMoves){
            let moves;
            let isCapture = false;

            if(pieceMove.moves.length > 0){
                moves = pieceMove.moves;
            }else{
                moves = pieceMove.captures;
                isCapture = true;
            }

            for(let move of moves){

                createNewNode(tempBf, pieceMove.piece, move, isCapture);
                let value = minmax(tempBf, depth-1, alpha, beta, tempBf.move)[1];

                if (value < bestScore){
                    bestScore = value;
                    bestMove = {src: pieceMove.piece, target: move, capture: isCapture};
                }
                beta = Math.min(beta, value);
                tempBf = tempBfClone(bf);
                if(alpha >= beta) break;
            }
            if(alpha >= beta) break;
        }
        return [bestMove, bestScore];
    }
}
```

FIGURE 1.8   Alpha-Beta pruning illustration.

its turn; a search algorithm is called which allows the program to look ahead at the possible future positions before deciding what move it wants to make in that current position. It's white turn to move now. In every move, there are only two possible moves to choose. We can visualize these moves as two separate branches at the end of which are two new positions, of course, it is black's turn to move now. We continue expanding these moves till either we reach the end of the game or we decide to stop because going deeper would take too much time. Either way, at the end of the tree we now have to perform the static evaluation on these final positions. The static evaluation means try to estimate how good the position is on one side without making any more moves. Large values would favor white and small values would favor black. For this reason, white constantly tries to maximize the evaluation hence known as the Maximizing player. In addition, black is always trying to minimize the evaluation, hence known as the Minimizing player. We start by evaluating the positions on the bottom left. In the previous position, it was white's turn to move, and since white will always choose the value that leads to the maximum evaluation, we assign the value to

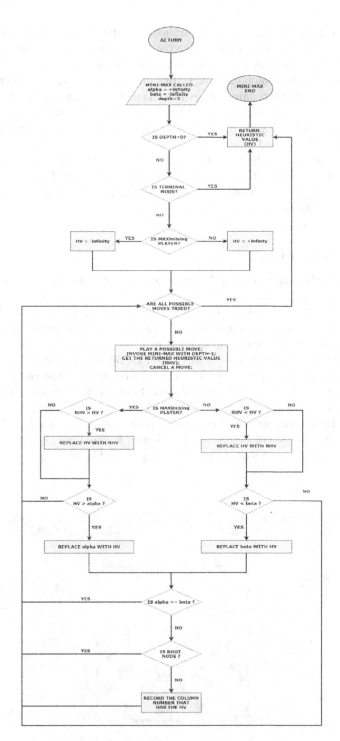

FIGURE 1.9 Flowchart depicting the implementation algorithm.

the node accordingly and complete the evaluation of that node using the right branch as well. Now, black will try to minimize the evaluation function, so we assign the position the lower value by comparing. In addition, we go up the tree hence returning the maximum-minimum gain and getting the higher probable position for white to move. This is where pruning comes into the picture. It would take a lot of time to go down all the branches to get the best value. Without exploring all the nodes through the branch, it tries to get the least or the max value from the already evaluated position. This would result in the player knowing that he already has a better option available and that he won't have to go down the other branch. These checks are made through Alpha-Beta parameters. This observation concludes that we don't have to waste any computation in evaluating the final position. Hence, we've pruned that position from the tree.

1.4.2 Graphical User Interface

The GUI is built using HyperText Markup Language (HTML) and Cascading Style Sheets (CSS). The primary reason for building the algorithm in JavaScript was due to the fact that it is one of the primary building blocks of web development. Therefore, the whole game is implemented as a web page. The board game is given a real checkerboard like feature to simulate real-time game playing making it visually more attractive as shown in Figures 1.10–1.13. Besides the board, the front end contains rules and tutorials so that the user with no previous knowledge can also play the game without any difficulty. A little brief about the history of checkers board is also mentioned so that the user can know about the origin of the checkers' game. Lastly information about chinook is also given. The rule-based features such as the upgradation of a piece into king is also depicted in a visually appealing form by depicting a crown on the piece (see Figures 1.14 and 1.15).

FIGURE 1.10   Before single capture of a piece.

FIGURE 1.11   After single capture of a piece.

FIGURE 1.12   Before multiple capture of pieces.

FIGURE 1.13   After multiple capture of pieces.

FIGURE 1.14   Upgradation of a piece into king on reaching the end side of the opponent.

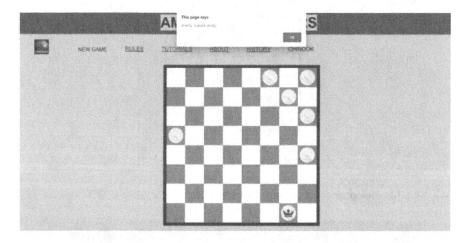

FIGURE 1.15   Displaying the result of the game.

1.5   UTILITY AND APPLICATION

The project is an implementation of a strategic board game checkers. It can be used to play checkers in an interactive environment. Figure 1.16 displays the use case flowchart of the project. The game's algorithm is developed using JavaScript which is one of the core technologies of web development. To provide a real-time playing simulation, the GUI of the game is built using HTML and CSS. The game is more accessible and user-friendly as it is built as a website. The frontend of the web page contains the instructions and rules of the game so that the user can play the game even without having any previous knowledge.

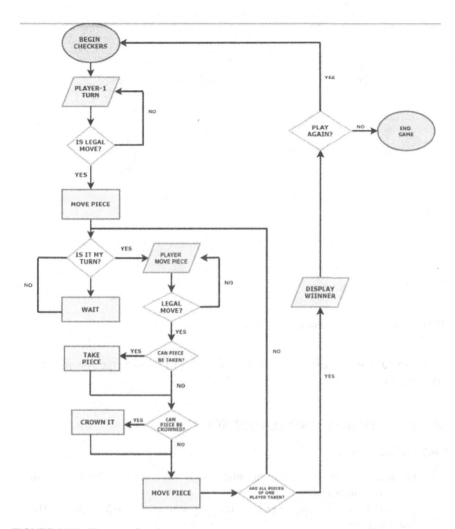

FIGURE 1.16 Use case flowchart.

The game is a one-player checkers game where the user can play with the AI and test their skills in strategic and logical gaming. Some benefits of playing checkers game are stated below:

- It develops concentration skills and promotes confident decision-making.
- It reduces stress and serves as a fun way to overcome boredom.
- It boosts problem-solving and pre-mathematics skills.

1.5.1 System Environment

By giving input, gamers will interact with the device (selecting the pieces and dragging them to the available tile). System produces the script with such inputs, if some change takes place (if the value is changed), the object is sent to render to display

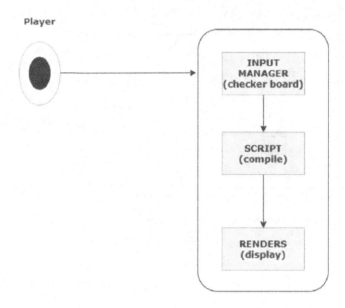

FIGURE 1.17   System environment diagram.

the content (a character can change its place). Figure 1.17 depicts the system environment diagram.

1.6   CONCLUSION AND FUTURE SCOPE

1.6.1   Conclusion

- The use of Minimax without optimization is not effective, although it can be a good solution with them.
- Alpha-Beta pruning improves exponentially with respect to Minimax as the range increases.
- Simple algorithms as a random player have no chance at depth greater than 1 against Alpha-Beta.
- There are several other solutions to *zero-sum* play, but Minimax with optimization using heuristic function and Alpha-Beta pruning tends to be a successful one.
- The introduction of different features will significantly boost heuristics.
- The depth of the game tree affects significantly the com-player quality.

1.6.2   Future Scope

- Different levels based on the depth of the tree can be introduced in the game such as easy, medium, and hard.
- Design a much more efficient heuristic function.
- Improve the GUI.

- Built a data management system to store the details of the user such as name, number of wins and losses.
- Add new features such as two-player games, different types of checkers.
- Using the same algorithms to make more two-player games such as tic-tac-toe and chess.

REFERENCES

1. Idzham, K., Khalishah, M., Steven, Y., Aminuddin, M.S., Syawani, H., Zain, A.M., and Yusoff, Y., Study of Artificial Intelligence into Checkers Game using HTML and JavaScript. IOP Conf. Ser.: Mater. Sci. Eng., 864, 012091, 2020. doi:10.1088/1757-899X/864/1/012091
2. Alkharusi, S., Checkers Research Paper Based on AI (2), 1, 7, 2020. https://www.researchgate.net/publication/339337169_checkers_research_paper_based_on_AI_2
3. Masters, J., Draughts, Checkers – Online Guide. www.tradgames.org.uk
4. Sutton R., Samuel's Checkers Player. In: Sammut C. and Webb G.I. (eds.), Encyclopedia of Machine Learning. Boston, MA: Springer, 2011. https://doi.org/10.1007/978-0-387-30164-8_740
5. Arthur, S., Some Studies in Machine Learning Using the Game of Checkers. IBM J. Res. Dev., 3 (3), 210–229, 1959. CiteSeerX 10.1.1.368.2254. doi:10.1147/rd.33.0210
6. Myerson, R., Game Theory: Analysis of Conflict. Cambridge, MA; London, England: Harvard University Press, p. 1, 1991. doi: 10.2307/j.ctvjsf522.15
7. Pearl, J., Heuristics: Intelligent Search Strategies for Computer Problem Solving. Reading, MA: Addison-Wesley Pub. Co., Inc., p. 3, 1984.OSTI 5127296.
8. Black, P. and Vreda, P., "Search Tree". Dictionary of Algorithms and Data Structures Figure 2. 2005. https://levelup.gitconnected.com/an-into-to-binary-search-trees-432f94d180da
9. Binmore, K., Playing for Real: A Text on Game Theory. New York, 2012. Oxford Scholarship Online: http://dx.doi.org/10.1093/acprof:osobl/9780199924530.001.0001
10. Kuo, Jonathan C.T., Artificial Intelligence at Play — Connect Four (Mini-max Algorithm Explained), 2020. https://medium.com/analytics-vidhya/artificial-intelligence-at-play-connect-four-minimax-algorithm-explained-3b5fc32e4a4f
11. Russell, S.J. and Peter, N., Artificial Intelligence: A Modern Approach (2nd ed.). Upper Saddle River, NJ: Prentice Hall, 2003, pp. 163–171. ISBN 0-13-790395-2 Figure 3: By Nuno Nogueira (Nmnoguera) http://en.wikipedia.org/wiki/Image:Minimax.svg, created in Inkscape by author, CC BY-SA 2.5, https://commons.wikimedia.org/w/index.php?curid=2276653d=2276653
12. Russell, S.J. and Norvig, P., Artificial Intelligence: A Modern Approach (3rd ed.). Upper Saddle River, NJ: Prentice Hall, 2010.
13. McCarthy, J., Human Level AI Is Harder Than It Seemed in 1955. 2005. Retrieved 2006-12-20.
14. Edwards, D.J. and Hart, T.P., The Alpha–Beta Heuristic (AIM-030). RLE and MIT Computation Center: Massachusetts Institute of Technology, 1961. hdl:1721.1/6098.
15. Knuth, D.E. and Moore, R.W., An Analysis of Alpha-Beta Pruning. Art. Intel., 6 (4), 293–326, 1975. doi:10.1016/0004-3702(75)90019-3 S2CID 7894372

2 The Future of Automatically Generated Animation with AI

Preety Khatri

CONTENTS

2.1 Introduction 19
2.2 Ai's Role in Animation 21
    2.2.1 How AI Replaces Animation 21
    2.2.2 Various Agents in AI 22
2.3 AI Latest Techniques in Animation 23
    2.3.1 Latest AI Technology 25
    2.3.2 AR Technology 26
    2.3.3 VR Technology 28
2.4 The Traditional and Modern Animation 30
    2.4.1 Traditional Animation 31
    2.4.2 Stop-Motion 32
    2.4.3 Modern Animation 33
2.5 Future Aspects of Animation with AI 33
2.6 Conclusion 34
References 35

2.1 INTRODUCTION

Computer animation refers to the addition of something new and improved to the conventional method of animation. A technique that uses a sequence of images in frames to create the illusion of movement. It is a technique that creates the illusion of movement by viewing images on a screen and capturing a sequence of individual states of an active scene using a recording device. An animation can be described as a movie made up of a series of rendered images. Various features such as file size, file format, frames per second (fps), compression, output size, and so on have been used to monitor the quality of the images in the picture or frames [1, 2]. The most popular form of animation is keyframing, in which the animation is generated at several points throughout the animation. At the same time, the computer creates all of the transition frames between the two keys. Changing the position, rotation, and scale of objects are all examples of animation techniques.

Setting the length of the animation in frames and fps is very important when animating. We can place the keys inside the frames with the aid of keyframes [3, 4].

To alter, transfer, rotate, or resize an object, the key is placed at the beginning and end of the desired path. Consider this scenario: if an object moves from point X to point Y in 4 seconds and you have 50 fps, put four keys 100 frames apart. Real-time animation allows you to give different objects physical properties. To control them, it employs a variety of controls and features. In the x, y, and z planes, you can create different objects, alter masses, create actors, control friction, and control forces. Architectural walk-throughs can be constructed using a variety of real-time animation and three-dimensional (3D) games.

There are two approaches to taking computer animation and evolution into account. The first approach involves combining traditional animation techniques with the use of a computer. The second approach focuses on simulation models based on physics and dynamics laws [5]. Consider the following scenario: Traditional methods allow us to build 3D characters with enhanced gestures, while simulation methods are used to model human actions accurately. Take bouncing balls, for example, where the motion of the balls can be enhanced by adding squash and stretch [3]. When an object is squashed, it expands and flattens out, indicating that it is made of a pliable and soft material. Various traditional animators use this tool. This does not provide a practical simulation, but it gives the audience an idea. A bouncing ball motion can also be fully simulated by computer using mechanics such as quantum conservation and Newton's laws, as shown in Figure 2.1 [2].

In the multimedia industry, autonomous virtual actors and real-time animation are critical because immersive use of functionality is a direct advantage. Each television and film producer will be eager to develop new programs and features to participate interactively [6]. Real-time animation capabilities are needed by editors, publishers, and writers of interactive TV programs, CD-ROMs, and CD-Is that are becoming increasingly interactive [3].

Computer animation has been regarded as a cutting-edge medium for visual effects (VFX) and advertising in films for many years. The rapid development of powerful super workstations in recent years has given rise to new areas such as video gaming, virtual reality (VR), and multimedia. The use of real-time animation and

FIGURE 2.1   Setting up keyframes for timing the bouncing balls.

digital technology has become a significant concern. The audience can only choose which programs to watch on traditional television [7]. With the latest advances in multimedia products and digital and interactive television, viewers will communicate with programming. This creation would pave the way for personalized programming for each viewer [6].

In animation, we can look at the following developments: computer animation began with very basic methods derived from conventional animation and keyframes [3]. There have also been developed several time-consuming rendering methods. Importing inverse dynamics and kinematics from robotics paves the way for more advanced simulation methods. Computer animation has traditionally focused on dynamic simulation and physics methods, particularly in collision detection and deformations [5].

With the advent of super workstations and VR applications, brute force approaches such as radioscopy are likely to resurface. In the future, real-time complex animation systems will be built using simulation and VR devices [8]. Autonomous actors and actual actors with motion captured by sensors are calculated by the machine using real-time behavioral simulation with complex physics-based interactions with the environment. Long-distance partners could be assigned to these dynamic scenes.

2.2 AI'S ROLE IN ANIMATION

Computers have left an indelible impression on art in a variety of ways. They may recognize their structures by recognizing pictures or photographs. On the other hand, computers affect animated videos or motion graphics because they have similarities with other pieces of similar work. The automatic engine gives its integrated software and base instructions [9].

A network that has been used for artificial intelligence (AI) is the phase feature neural. As a result, AI is being used to make humans seem more realistic in animated films and video games. However, it is improving at a faster rate than most animators. The impressiveness of the AI takeover of this new invention can be attributed to the animation's accuracy. However, there has been much backlash against individual creative expression. When speaking with real animators about the case, for example [10].

Art is a type of human speech that is subjective. As a result, when a machine takes away the fundamental concept of creative expression, society feels challenged. This non-human entity is challenging to have in a space that was not designed for it, and if AI continues to advance, humanity could be in grave danger. Even if none of it reverberates with the public, they would prefer to animate and build [11]. This is why the inventors have proposed that AI be limited to the function of association, where it will alter and improve processes while allowing humans to influence creative production and design.

2.2.1 How AI Replaces Animation

Nowadays, technology has replaced many occupations, including creatives, resulting in a dynamic job market. The animators are the creatives who are obsessed with their work. Their talent appears to be on the verge of a significant change, as with most workers, which are both boring and menial. To engage in such activities, most people need some motivation. Inventors use technology to make their lives simpler in any way. There are already computers and appliances that perform our every-day tasks, such as washing machines and microwaves. There are several automation tools available that can perform most of the tasks that animators can perform with AI. As a result, we can conclude that AI is now the most dominant industry and that technology is performing better than humans [12].

2.2.2 Various Agents in AI

One of the most critical areas in AI is agent, which is primarily concerned with intelligent systems [13]. In terms of AI, an agent is a machine that exists in a given environment and makes its own decisions. It uses sensors to perceive the environment and actuators to function in the environment. Intelligent agents, robotics, and other technologies are examples.

As seen in Figure 2.2, which shows how autonomous agents are classified. The term "real-life agents" refers to living animals such as mammals, reptiles, fish, and birds. Robotic agents of the mechanical kind, on the other hand, are also agents from the AI perspective—for example, the robot rovers used for NASA's Mars Rover missions. Computer agents are agents that only exist in a virtual or web-based world [10].

Agents that process human language, agents that gather various information, agents that are informative, agents that are intelligent and learn, and agents that are programmed for a specific purpose such as entertainment, e.g., in games, special VFX, 3D animation, and so on are all examples of software agents. Software agents

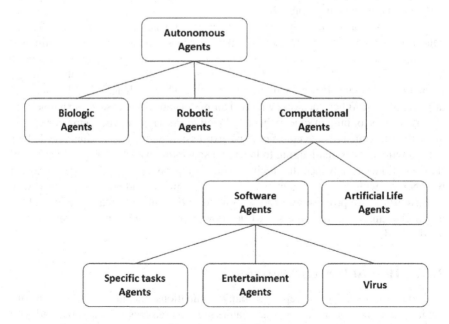

FIGURE 2.2 Classification of autonomous agents.

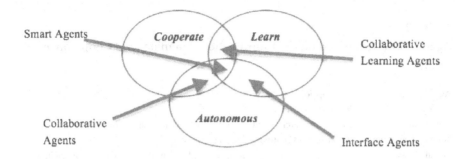

FIGURE 2.3 A topology of agent.

and artificial life agents are examples of computational agents. Computer agents are further classified as quest agents, learning agents, preparation agents, conversational, intelligent agents, and so on [13].

Figure 2.3 shows a topology of intelligent agents, collaborative agents, collaborative learning agents, and interface agents based on their learning, coordination, autonomy, and other characteristics. Agents function at a higher level than symbols and require high-level communications.

Agents use a variety of bots, including chatterbots, which are used for web chatting. Annoybots, which are used to disrupt chat rooms and newsrooms. Spambots, which are used to generate junk mails after collecting web email addresses. Mail bots, which are used to manage and filter email, and spider bots, which are used to scrape content from the internet.

As a result of the above, we may conclude that agents are those who act or exert force. Anything that produces or is capable of producing an effect is referred to as an agent. An agent is allowed to act for or in the role of another person, such as a government delegate, emissary, or official who engages in undercover activities; it may also be a business representative, as shown in Table 2.1 [14]. Based on the coordination, planning, and cooperative ability, the agent's properties can be classified as:

2.3 AI LATEST TECHNIQUES IN ANIMATION

Adobe has introduced the most recent techniques, which include 3D object movement, morphing, kinetics, and the addition of voice recording. It took some time for this skill to build. It restricts what a human animator can accomplish [15]. Most of these mediums are being reformed and expanded, which has enormous potential. In the case of network traffic, about 60% of it originates from internet-connected computers. Animation videos demonstrate the effectiveness and productivity of the animation industry, which is growing in terms of conversion rate and variety [1]. There are many ways to understand how AI helps animators. The following are some of the features:

- *Better Workflow*: AI can help animation studios enhance communication by improving essential functions: the strategy development and decision-making process for the AI-assisted project. The essential advantage is that

TABLE 2.1

Agent Properties Based on the Coordination, Planning, and Cooperative Ability

Agent Property	Description
Ability to set goals	The agent has a purpose
Autonomy	The agent exercises control over its actions and run asynchronously
Temporal continuity	The agent is a continuity running process
Social ability	The agent can communicate in a complex manner with other agents, including people, in order to obtain information
Proactivity	The agent responds in the best possible way to possible future actions that are anticipated to happen
Reactivity	The agent responds in a timely fashion to changes in the environment and decides for itself when to act
Versatility	The agent can have multiple goals at the same time
Persistency	The agent will continue steadfastly in pursuit of any plan
Rationality	The agent makes rational, informed decisions
Mobility	The agent can transport itself around its environment

managers can make better choices in their workflows and activities as a result [16].

- *The Ideas about Streamlining*: Customer support and chatbots are programmed to work together in the same way that humans do. These digital portals are appealing in terms of improved communication methods and changing the way artists think about their projects. The dedication entails putting concepts and thoughts associated with projects on hold before an incredible new concept emerges. Not only can it be saved without human intervention with the aid of the virtual assistant, but it will also be achieved more effectively due to the artist's simple mind frame.

- *Information Control*: Regularly, animators work with a large number of different types of data. Animators must consider coloring, set design, motion graphics, and scale charts within a single picture. This info, which serves as a digital assistant for artists, is now handled by AI technology. Prioritization of urgent texts, instructions, and the importance of style accessible to designers so that they can focus on their specific tasks. In creative settings, this hands-on assistance approach has proven to be highly beneficial [17].

- *Diminishing Workload*: Experts agree that AI has significantly reduced workload, allowing developers to have lighter workloads. Voice-activated personal assistants like Alexa and Siri are assisting animators in doing their jobs more effectively. AI is now taking over business activities that are not part of the creative process [14]. Artists can be more creative and perform smarter as a result of this. Since AI follows scripted paths, the animator's artistic integrity is not jeopardized.

- *Patterns Prediction*: The chatbots will be designed to have honest conversations using machine learning (ML). With the help of Alexa or Google, this nonlinear advantage will allow predictions about employee preferences and workplace trends. The virtual assistant is evolving into an actual assistant capable of answering complicated questions about production and design. The animators avoid tedious study activities while keeping their previous work organized and saved for future reference [8].

AI algorithms will easily do data-driven work without taking up the time that people might. This new technology can now accomplish what teams of animators will take weeks to accomplish. AI's true success is making seamless edits, nuanced characterization, and significant VFX, in addition to providing a solid track record. Even though these algorithms are very costly and are used by large companies such as Disney. The animators are uncertain about their future careers as a result of this.

To make human lives more straightforward, the tricky part is that not every artist contributes to this mentality. If not alarming, the intrusion of technology into their artistic work is frustrating. Filmmakers have not yet captured the entire AI movement where these training devices are present to generate worlds and animations. This is primarily due to a lack of communication between the filmmaker and the invention.

2.3.1 LATEST AI TECHNOLOGY

As we all know, digital technology is rapidly evolving. We use various new technology regularly, such as voice assistant Alexa, Siri, Google Maps, and so on. AI in animation is currently being developed and used to some degree by animators to speed up time-consuming tasks. One of the key benefits of using AI to automate those stages in animation [18] is that you have more time to focus on other activities when you speed things up.

Companies like Adobe have already developed features for their standard animate suite that connect up characters' mouth movements to sound. Moreover, others are going even further by leveraging AI to create solutions that completely automate characters' movements and facial expressions as they speak, based on data collected through ML, effectively automating this delicate, time-consuming task.

When it comes to cutting-edge technology, ML is one of the AI systems in which computers are not directly programmed to perform those tasks. Instead, they automatically learn and develop as a result of their experiences. Deep learning is a form of ML that uses artificial neural networks to make predictions. Unsupervised learning, supervised learning, and reinforcement learning are examples of ML algorithms.

The algorithm in unsupervised learning does not use personal data to work on it without any guidance. It deduces a function from the training data, which consists of collecting an input object and the desired output in supervised learning. Machines use reinforcement learning to take appropriate actions to maximize the incentive in order to find the best option that should be considered.

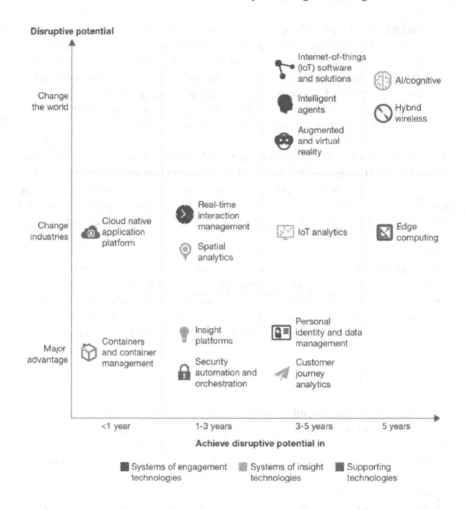

FIGURE 2.4 Five emerging technologies that will change the world in next five years. (Source: Forrester Research, Inc., unauthorized production, citation, or distribution prohibited.)

As seen in Figure 2.4, five new technologies will change the world in the next five years. Based on parameters including systems of engagement technologies, systems of insight technologies, and supporting technologies [19], various emerging technologies such as Internet of Things (IoT), virtual and augmented reality (VR and AR), hybrid wireless, AI/cognitive, intelligent agents, real-time interaction management, spatial analytics, cloud-native application frameworks, insight platforms, and so on have been elaborated in this figure.

2.3.2 AR TECHNOLOGY

In AR systems, the consumer wears a head-mounted display (HMD) and uses a device, which involves many boundaries. The H/w was bulky, and the HMD interfered with the user's standard view [20]. It is also susceptible to causing discomforts such as dizziness or nausea. As a result, the performance of the AR systems on that particular hardware necessitated a significant amount of effort and time from the developers. These drawbacks have been alleviated by the appearance and rapid evolution of smartphones. There are variously powerful smartphones on the market based on HMD's technology. As a result, the consumer does not have to keep the hardware and their versatility is enhanced. As a result, there is now various smartphone AR applications available on the market that digital layer knowledge over the physical world [21].

We can see the digital data visible with the aid of a smartphone camera and position it in a specific location. Knowledge may be positioned in a variety of ways, including by the use of a mobile device. The new smartphones have Global Navigation Satellite System (GNSS) orientation sensors, localization systems, and other features. The orientation sensor processes the unprocessed sensor data from the accelerometer to obtain information. The orientation sensor provides pitch (degrees of rotation about the x-axis) and roll (degrees of rotation about the y-axis). As a result, the device's direction is determined by the pitch and roll values. When a smartphone is positioned at a specific location with known coordinates and orientation, the digital information is visualized using the camera. The accuracy of the GNSS positioning is a disadvantage of this system.

The accuracy of the signal decreases in areas with tall buildings or a large number of trees, and the signal bounces off. Furthermore, this device is ineffective inside houses. The use of markers is a different way of displaying digital data. A marker is a square frame with a light-colored, usually white, center and a dark-colored, usually black, outer frame [22]. Each marker is made using a unique pattern, making them one-of-a-kind. In the marker recognition process, the smartphone camera gathers and processes images in real-time intending to identify a pattern. The color detection, known shapes, repeated and geometries patterns image recognition techniques are focused on finding patterns of color detection, known shapes, repeated and geometries patterns.

When a creator is discovered, the virtual knowledge on the camera overlaps. Natural feature tracking (NFT) is a technique that uses artifacts or pictures instead of markers to monitor natural features. As a result, NFT enables users to recognize and monitor natural features on objects and images. Digital data such as two-dimensional (2D) images, 3D models, video, audio, text, animation, etc. This opens up the possibility of developing a wide range of applications, such as:

1. In the case of ads, it is often used to promote new goods online.
2. In entertainment and education, AR helps develop cultural learning games (educational aim games).
3. In medicine, AR applications are being created to help surgeons achieve a minimally invasive operation with increased dexterity, precision, and visualization.

It is now much easier to create AR applications. The primary advantage is that anyone can build applications for similar hardware. This allows for the best app

TABLE 2.2

Summary of AR Frameworks

	Location-Based	Operating System	NFT	Marker-Based
Droid AR	x	Android	----------	X
AR Toolkit	-----------	iOS, Android, Linux, Windows, Mac OS X, Unity 3D	x	X
Beyond AR	x	Android	---------	------------
Vuforia	-----------	Android, iOS, Unity 3D	x	X
Mixer	-----------	Android & iPhone	x	X

progress [20] due to many growing software structures. A framework usually provides some basic features that can be used to build more complex applications. The most significant advantage of using outlines is that they include general application structure, they aid developer relationships, and many available resources and libraries can be used for frameworks. There are many platforms available these days for quickly creating AR applications [21].

Table 2.2 summarizes the existing state of free AR framework functionality. Many structures are no longer maintained, and as a result, the list is constantly changing. AR Toolkit and Vuforia are the most user-friendly and comprehensive tools, but if you want to build a position-based app, you will need to use one of the other frameworks [2].

2.3.3 VR TECHNOLOGY

Even though AR and VR are closely linked technologies, they all depict peculiar realities. When we talk about AR, we are talking about adding elements to reality, while VR creates a new reality that is not actual. VR is an artificial world developed with specialized software. VR displays a 3D image that can be explored interactively using controls such as a game console, a computer mouse, or sensor-equipped gloves [23].

VR systems include using a HMD, such as glasses, to learn about the virtual world. The first VR device had poor graphics quality and needed a complicated HMD. The HMD has advanced dramatically in recent years, and there are now regulating solutions on the market, such as Oculus Rift. Oculus VR [7] is working on a VR headset similar to the Oculus Rift.

Stereoscopic vision is used in the treatment. Stereoscopic vision is a method of gathering 3D visual information that gives a picture the illusion of depth. Due to their separation, the eyes in natural stereo vision generated two images with minor variations between them. To construct depth perception, the brain processes these variations. The HMD projects a stereoscopic view. Two images are shown on the projector, one for each eye. A small controller is used to monitor the interpupillary distance based on the display.

Individuals and elements vary in their eye separation, resulting in a realistic stereoscopic vision-logic. The HMD function and sensors that monitor the user's head movements and change the picture are known as a virtual surround sound system.

For the time being, this gadget will connect your machine to your smartphone. Some users report experiencing headaches or motion sickness as a result of the immersive 3D vision. To avoid this, it is necessary to adjust the lens to each individual's vision. However, prolonged use can cause anxiety.

Imagining VR with an HMD is a little annoying at times. However, creating a semi-immersive app in which a 3D model is shown on the smartphone monitor seems promising. Throughout the touch screen, the user will collaborate with it. Users can load 3D models and collaborate with them using those frameworks. These frameworks can be used to build simple semi-immersive applications. However, if you want to work with 3D models for animations, rendering, and other purposes, a game engine is the best choice.

A software framework is a game engine developed for the production and creation of video games that can be played on a variety of platforms. Loading, rendering, object collision detection, animation, physics, inputs, graphical user interface (GUI), and AI are the engine's key components. The game engine also has other tools for creating the actual game, such as terrains, characters, real-world object behaviors, and so on. The game engine includes all of the resources needed to create a VR app. Many game engines also support stereoscopic vision [24].

Mind3d, a lightweight 3D framework for Android based on OpenGL ES v1.0/1.1, is one of the several 3D model frameworks available. This system includes tools for loading and modifying.m2d, 3ds, and. Obj files. It cannot be sustained at this time. The disadvantage is that these previously mentioned frameworks are only compatible with Android, making it difficult for beginner programmers to create apps. On the other hand, the game engine is the best way to build a virtual world and expand basic functionality.

Unreal Engine 4, CryEngine, and Unity are the most common game engines at the moment. These game engines are prevalent, and although each has its own set of advantages and disadvantages, they are all compatible with VR glasses [25]. Unity is the simplest to use and is compatible with all mobile devices, but the graphics quality is lower, and real-time simulation is impossible.

Unreal Engine 4 has incredible graphics capabilities, allowing for the development of hyper-realistic scenes, but it is only compatible with iOS and Android. However, it is easy to use. Finally, because of the engine's steep learning curve, CryEngine is better suited to experienced developers, though the graphics quality is excellent. The main characteristics of these game engines are summarized in Table 2.3 [25].

TABLE 2.3
A Summary of Game Engines

	Mobile Platforms	Languages Support	Other Platforms
Unity	Android, iOS, Windows	JavaScript, C#, Boo	PC, PlayStation, Xbox, Wii, 3DS, VR, TV, Web
Unreal Engine 4	Android, iOS	C++	PC, PlayStation, Xbox, VR
CryEngine [25]		C++, Lua, C#	PC, PlayStation, Xbox, VR

2.4 THE TRADITIONAL AND MODERN ANIMATION

The illusion of movement and extrude in a speedy display of a series of still, static images with slight vast modifications is the technical concept of what generalized animation is. Since its first appearance in France, animation has come a long way in a short period. The primary known second of excellent animated film in records on the Musee Grevin is projecting the first lively excellent animated film in Paris's Theatre Optique. Since then, animation has grown into a massive industry with a diverse range of art styles, techniques, a significant starting point for storytelling, technological advancements, job opportunities in design and animation, and much more. The list could go on and on.

We had to go back to the beginnings of how live-action movies first became popular, and we looked at it in the same way we looked at the beginnings of traditional art, i.e., cave paintings. Hand-drawn drawings and movie rolls have become the opposites of traditional art's cave paintings in animation.

Sketches, drawings, paintings, and practically any handcrafted recognizable piece created with worldly bodily materials made up of traditional animation. When the world's first full-length animated feature film, *Snow White and the Seven Dwarfs*, was released in 1937, a few years after Walt Disney's 1928 *Steamboat Willie* cartoon, no one could have predicted how famous, and influential this new type of entertainment would become in the years to come.

When *Toy Story* was released in 1995, it was the first computer-generated mental imagery film. Not only did ancient invigorating patterns blend with digital medium models, but Hollywood produced such a significant flip. Computer-generated imagery (CGI) films, on the other hand, were a massive success with audiences after that. A significant new investment for big-name studios with big budgets, as well as an opportunity for animators to try out new mediums. Thousands of people will have new work and career prospects.

CGI creates animated images using computer graphics that use both dynamic and static images to generate scenes. Though computer animation consists solely of moving images, the technical concept of View CGI is another amazing way to explore new styles of art and storytelling through miles of data on an electric operating system. The current controversy about whether conventional or digital animation is superior is only partially true.

It is because many people overlook the significance of the two. It is similar to understanding the distinction between video and animation. The physical and virtual differences in the room, equipment, and materials are a simple statement [11]. The video consists of the anatomy of movement into individual images, while animation starts with individual images that are then shaped together to produce the illusion of continuous.

Traditional animation requires a story that should and will always be valued, loved, and cherished, as it is the foundation for all forms of animation. It does not matter whether we are talking about digital, stop-motion, chuckimation, puppetry, claymation, sand animation, typography, painting on glass, drawing on film, or something else. Because of all of these various animation styles, we would have come from making this point legitimate to be divisive, but it is absurd to pick one side or claim one is better than the other [4].

It is the equivalent of ignoring the roots of animation and film, which are traditional art and photography. Both are intertwined and would not exist without the advancement of technology and artistic movements. Computer animation is why so many people are upset to be protective because it is a different way for thousands of artists, designers, and engineers to have more freedom to work that is cared for your likeness, not just that it is a more open and structural workflow.

When it comes down to it, it is all about personal preference. It might also come down to what is best for the project. People should consider that creating digital animations opens up a world of possibilities and access that conventional animation cannot match.

For instance, having various controls in any environment where you want to work physically and artistically is a good example. Only animation studios had the physical resources to create and screen animated films. Anyone now has unrestricted access to make an animated film and distribute it as they see fit. Because of all the possibilities for animating [9], the field is far more available in terms of creativity. There is no way to animate in a single way or a single form. It is shocking when someone criticizes it because it is so extensive and accessible.

Whether 2D or 3D is better nowadays has almost nothing to do with technological properties, but instead with which one can work better. Recently, there have been some fantastic 2D films, such as *Iron Giant* and *Lilo & Stitch*, as well as some terrifying 3D films, such as *Final Fantasy*. *Spirit*, *Treasure Planet*, and *Sinbad* failed simply because they were terrible movies in plot and pacing, not because of the medium in which they were produced. And some of the most popular 3D films include *Shark Tale* (2003), *Planes* (2013), *Norm of the North* (2016), and *Alpha and Omega* (2010). Essentially, 3D is yet another method to aid in the filmmaking process. We use it and want to use it to be most appropriate for the project, but the medium does not determine the result. Ideas, pencils, and paper are the best starting points for a film. The way you play your story has a significant impact on its success. What best suits the project is decided by finding out the suitable media and resources that will work with the story.

At this point in the history of animation and its technology, having the best of all worlds, physical and digital, is critical. Technology has simply moved into a more modern reality. However, it has rarely replaced key elements that capture the heart of animation, which many people fear when they believe technology is about to make a significant shift in any field.

Many people are afraid of being replaced one day by a computer or someone who has the tools to do three jobs for one low price.

To counter this misconception, there will always be new employment that will most likely replace old ones, yes. However, it will also lead to more creative content in other fields that defiantly require the physical labor of a human mind. Suppose the future doesn't manage to invent a computer with such an advanced artificial mind to produce fantastic animation without being villains someday. In that case, we will have something to be concerned about [17].

2.4.1 TRADITIONAL ANIMATION

Traditional animation is also known as hand-drawn animation or classic animation. Each frame is hand-drawn on a physical medium in this animation technique. This technology was prevalent in the cinema before the advent of computers. A sequence of sketches on transparent pages is used to create this animation technique. Traditional animation starts with the creation of a plot. Following the selection of the plot, the artist creates a storyboard that resembles a comic book [4]. The storyboard depicts the filming sequences of camera angles and frames. Before the director approves a scene in the storyboard stage, the animator may need to repeat it several times.

Traditional animators work in batches, drawing one picture or frame at a time. In conventional animation, the pencil is the primary weapon. Artist creates a drawing on a sheet of transparent paper that can be inserted into your desk's connector strip. The peg bar is a traditional animation method used to hold drawings in place. The artist creates the character solely with a pencil, which is then shot or scanned and synced with the necessary soundtracks. Before the animation is sent to the supervisors, the artist will check and develop his work [4].

Each pencil-drawn frame of the animation is transferred to the animation. Background images are painted and superimposed on cels, cels, or celluloid pages. Background artists typically paint the sets on which the animated sequence's action takes place. Acrylic paint was commonly used to create the backdrop: animators study models, dolls, puppets, real-life figures for inspiration. The main animator in an animation studio creates a character's key or mainframes [4]. Twining is a technique in which the primary animator draws the main points of the action while the junior animator completes the intermediate or incomplete frames.

The animator uses keyframes to monitor the movement of the character's arms, eyes, and mouth. A supervisor animator, a small group of leading animators, and many assistant animators work together in a large budget animation production group. Key animators decide the main action of the character. After that, the accepted pencil animation graphics are photographed with a black and white animation camera.

Traditional animation includes 2D cell animation and stop-motion animation, even though both can use digital recording techniques in the end. The process used to create the animation is what matters most. Cell animation typically includes hand drawing, hand inking, and hand painting each structure on actual paper and cells. At the same time, stop-motion involves dealing with physical designs and objects shot with the camera one frame at a time. You get your simple cartoon movie, like Mulan, with traditional animation. It is a method of drawing pictures, photographing them, and then animating them so that the original drawings are slightly different.

2.4.2 STOP-MOTION

Stop-motion animation has been a staple of film special effects for almost as long as films have existed. Stop-motion animation is an enjoyable and straightforward animation technique. Even if you do not know it, you have probably seen stop-motion animation in advertisements, music videos, TV shows, and movies. Although it is popular to think of stop-motion as a single form [12], it is not. Stop-motion techniques can create a wide variety of film forms, not just sound animation. You are on your way if you combine parallel parts of digital camera, machine, and imagination. Though computer-generated animation is more flashy, stop-motion animation has its own rich culture.

2.4.3 MODERN ANIMATION

The effect is created electronically using either 2D or 3D models in computer animation. Virtualization of the traditional 2D animation workspace is ordinary in 2D computer animation, taking pen and paper into the digital realm to redesign cartoon animation types and workflows. 3D computer animation workflows usually mix conventional timelines and workflows adapted to work in 3D virtual space [2].

In any case, you are dealing with computer animation if you are animating on video. Avatar and Antz, for example, contain 3D animation, while Cartoon Network and Nickelodeon will use 2D for the majority of their cartoon features. Pixar's animation style is 3D computer animation. It entails animating with computers in a 3D world.

Computer graphics and animation are now used in almost every audiovisual media, from movies to commercials. This is so that objects, environments, and characters can be created that would be impossible or difficult to construct in actual life animation. It has now become an integral part of our everyday lives. It is used for movies, education, and a variety of other commercial purposes.

2.5 FUTURE ASPECTS OF ANIMATION WITH AI

Since many experts are scrutinizing ML and AI, it is only logical that their implementation is explained at a basic level. Only by incorporating AI into unique areas of everyday life will animators and video makers embrace this new AI era. The usage of smartphones and the advent of the new millennium after the tumultuous 1990s are two examples. Engineers, designers, and actors will understand the neural network and use it in their creative processes as soon as these types of applications appear [19].

The day does not come as soon as we spend too much time in a movie theater watching a film that AI, performed by robots, conceptualized and animated using deep learning algorithms. Because of the AI-powered animation automation, it is reasonable to assume that algorithms, AI software, and robots will begin to dominate the industry, based on their approach to factories and, as a result, customer service tasks [26].

Some may even consider the Associate in animation advice to be an art form. Some tasks should no longer be performed manually, and that AI can easily automate, but there is a greater need for qualified people to train deep learning algorithms. Routine tasks, such as creating a digital character, would encourage creative artists to spend less time on the time-consuming frame-by-frame method of writing and instead focus on more exciting things. So that animators do not have to draw frame by frame, AI automates animation-only tasks. Advanced AI-based algorithms can automate the rendering of advanced VFX.

As shown in Figure 2.5, which shows opportunities in the 3D animation market. From the analysis, we can summarize that:

- The global 3D animation market is projected to expand at a compound annual growth rate (CAGR) of 11.9 percent during the precast era, from USD 12,010 million in 2017 to USD 21,050 million in 2022 [17].

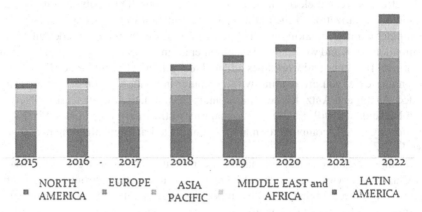

3D Animation Market (USD Million)

2015   2016 · 2017   2018   2019   2020   2021   2022

NORTH   EUROPE   ASIA   MIDDLE EAST and   LATIN
AMERICA   PACIFIC   AFRICA   AMERICA

FIGURE 2.5 Attractive opportunities in the 3D animation market. (Source: Markets and markets analysis.)

- Increased use of VFX technology and 3D applications in media and games and 3D imagery mapping and geospatial coordinates are driving market development.
- Market growth is attributed to the increasing use of VFX technology and #D application in media and games and 3D imaging in mapping and geospatial coordinates.
- The emergence of VR and AI technologies provides growth opportunities for the 3D animation market [23].
- Emerging economics in various regions, such as APAC, offer new opportunities.

2.6 CONCLUSION

The future of automatically generated animation with AI was addressed in this chapter. The effect of AI on animation and how modern animation differs from traditional animation are discussed in this chapter [8]. This chapter examines whether AI can replace animators in animation, which is a significant concern these days.

The latest technologies for 3D models were discussed in this chapter, and these technologies provide users with authentic and enriching experiences when visualizing 3D objects. Some users may be bothered and inconvenienced by these apps, especially those that require the use of VR glasses. As a result, some users can prefer AR apps or using the mobile screen to view 3D models [27].

As AI technology improves and spreads across the industry, animators, filmmakers, and designers are jumping in and making high-quality animations with fewer people in less time. AI is also having a positive effect on animation and motion graphics, pushing the boundaries of what can be done with animation. Disney is known for using AI to create storyboard animations solely from scripts that include terms like "turn right" and make the character turn in that direction in the animation.

The first move is to build a photorealistic 3D model. Image-based photogrammetric techniques may be used to create complex and extensive models. Nonetheless, the resulting point clouds are so large that the hardware of a cell phone does not support them. As a result, optimizing 3D models is critical if photorealistic models for smartphone apps are developed. VR and AI technologies are paving the way for potential growth in the 3D animation industry [23].

REFERENCES

1. Agrawal, A., Joshua G., and Avi G. eds., Introduction to: "Economics of Artificial Intelligence." In Economics of Artificial Intelligence. Toronto: nber.org, 2018. http://www.nber.org/chapters/c14005.pdf.
2. Funge J., Making Them Behave: Cognitive Models for Computer Animation, Ph.D. thesis, Department of Computer Science, University of Toronto, 1998.
3. Burtnyk N, and Wein M., Computer-generated Keyframe Animation, J. SMPTE, 80, 149–153, 1971.
4. Lasseter J., Principles of Traditional Animation Applied to 3D Computer Animation, Proc. SIGGRAPH '87, Computer Graphics, 21 (4), 35–44, 1987.
5. Amiguet-Vercher J., Szarowicz A., and Forte P., Synchronized Multi-agent Simulations for Automated Crowd Scene Simulation, AGENT-1 Workshop Proc., IJCAI, 1, 4–10, 2001.
6. Mayer, R.E., and Moreno, R., Animation as an Aid to Multimedia Learning. Educational Psych Rev., 14 (1), 87–99, 2002.
7. CSIRO Mathematical and Information Sciences (n.d.), Virtual Reality for Teaching Anatomy and Surgery, 2004. Retrieved from http://www.siaa.asn.au/docs/CSIROscopestudy.pdf.
8. Boden, M.A., AI: Its Nature and Future. Oxford, New York: Oxford University Press, 2016.
9. Park O.C., and Gittelman S.S., Selective use of Animation and Feedback in Computer-based Instruction, Educ. Technol. Res. Dev., 40, 27–38, 1992.
10. Fikes R., and Nilsson, N., STRIPS: A New Approach to the Application of Theorem Proving to Problem-Solving, Artif. Intell., 2, 189–208, 1971.
11. Milheim, W.D., How to Use Animation in Computer-assisted Learning, Br. J. Educ. Technol., 24 (3), 171–178, 1993.
12. Palmer, S., and Elkerton, J., Animated Demonstrations for Learning Procedural Computer-based Tasks, Hum. Comput. Interact., 8, 193–216, 1993.
13. Funge J., Tu X., and Terzopoulos D., Cognitive Modeling: Knowledge, Reasoning, and Planning for Intelligent Characters. Computer Graphics Proceedings: SIGGRAPH 99, 1999.
14. Bass, A.S., Non-Tech Businesses Are Beginning to Use Artificial Intelligence. Financial Times, 2018.
15. Rieber, L.P., Animation as Feedback in Computer-Based Simulation: Representation Matters, Educ. Technol. Res. Dev., 44, 5–22, 1996.
16. Long D., The AIPS-98 Planning Competition, AI Mag., 21 (2), pp 13–33, 2000.
17. Reynolds C.W., Computer Animation with Scripts and Actors, Proc. SIGGRAPH'82, 289–296, 1982.
18. Russell S., and Norvig P., Artificial Intelligence, A Modern Approach. London: Prentice-Hall, 1999.
19. Tversky, B., Morrison, J. B., and Bétrancourt M., Animation: Can it facilitate?, Int. J. Hum. Comput. Stud., 57, 247–262, 2002.
20. ARTOOLKIT, Open source augmented reality SDK. Artoolkit.org, 2016. [online] Available from: http://artoolkit.org.

21. Carmigniani, J., Furht, B., An Isetti, M., Ceravolo, P., Damiani, E., and Ivkovic, M., Augmented Reality Technologies, Systems, and Applications, Multimedia Tools Appl., 51 (1), 341–377, 2011.

22. Schnotz, W., Böckheler, J., and Grzondziel, H., Individual and Cooperative Learning with Interactive Animated Pictures, Eur. J. Psychol. Ed., 14, 245–265, 1999.

23. Beier K.P., Virtual Reality: A Short Introduction, 2004. Retrieved from http://www-vrl. umich.edu/intro/.

24. Zeltzer D., Towards an Integrated View of 3D Computer Animation, The Visual Computer, 1 (4), 249–259, 1985.

25. CRYENGINE. Cryengine. 2016. [online] Available from: https://www.cryengine.com/ features.

26. Fikes R., Hart, P., and Nilsson, N., Learning and Executing Generalized Robot Plans, Art. Intell., 3, 251–288, 1972.

27. Draganov, I.R. and Boumbarov, O.L., Investigating Oculus Rift Virtual Reality Display Applicability to Medical Assistive System for Motor Disabled Patients. The 8th IEEE International Conference, 2015.

3 Artificial Intelligence as Futuristic Approach for Narrative Gaming

*Toka Haroun, Vikas Rao Naidu,
and Aparna Agarwal*

CONTENTS

3.1 Introduction 37
3.2 Related Works..38
    3.2.1 AI for Computer Games 38
    3.2.2 AI for Adaptive Computer Games..41
    3.2.3 AI in Video Games: Toward a Unified Framework..........................41
    3.2.4 Narrative in Video Games 42
    3.2.5 Narrative Game Mechanics 43
    3.2.6 Interactive Narrative 44
    3.2.7 Adventure Games and Puzzle Design 44
    3.2.8 The Horror Genre and Video Games 45
3.3 Player Experience 48
3.4 Methodologies used in Game Development 51
3.5 AI Elements in the Proposed Narrative Gaming Model 58
3.6 Q-Algorithm for AI in Gaming 60
3.7 Conclusion 62
References..62

3.1 INTRODUCTION

Artificial intelligence (AI) in video games comprises the systems designed and developed to create the choices and actions of non-player characters (NPC) within a game. Video games that are developed currently, deliver an awfully fascinating ground for testing and researching new ideas for AI. These games integrate diverse and detailed environments with systems that are developed to allow dynamic, complex, and smart real-time choices. In various video game genres such as strategy, action, and role-playing games, the NPC are developed to have a rule-based system with variations according to different scenarios. However, machine learning (ML) methods are sometimes applied to allow NPC to adapt and learn from their interaction with the player character according to their success or failure. Although ML can be used to improve the NPC's overall performance, it is not usually applied in video games.

DOI: 10.1201/9781003231530-3

Social isolation measures due to COVID-19 has affected many people especially young adults causing loss of a sense of community, negative impacts on learning and development, and increase in impersonality (Sikali, 2020). Computer games can offer entertainment and stress relief during the pandemic (Ferguson, 2020).

Narrative and storytelling games can help players in social isolation by offering an immersive storytelling experience where the player can explore and interact with the game environment to reveal the plot of the game.

This research is aimed at helping people during social isolation especially young adults with emotional wellbeing (Anderton Kevin, 2018). Providing the players with an immersive experience that is unlikely to be experienced in the real world, where the players need to solve puzzles and explore a thrilling and mysterious environment from the safety of their homes (Butler, 2016).

This chapter will also contribute to the independent game development community by using the recent studies and tools in game development to create an immersive storytelling experience for player that is accessible online.

Acquiescent to gaming objectives of AI, generally seven goals or on target by the game developers for delivering an enjoyable and thrilling gaming experience to the players:

1. **Unpredictable behavior:** The game moves should not be predictable by the players.
2. **Cheating should not be allowed:** AI in games must be dynamic devoid of trickery.
3. **Utilizing the game surroundings:** AI in the game should make use of the game surroundings in a smart manner, such that no characteristic of the environment goes untraceable or unutilized.
4. **Imagination:** novel solutions should be generated by the game AI for unanticipated game situations.
5. **Apparent inferior behavior:** AI in games should not reveal evident substandard behavior against the player, reason being not to be easily defeated by the player.
6. **Identical human behavior:** The behavior displayed by game AI should be comparable in intricacy to the human behavior.
7. **Self-correction:** To prevent the mistakes being repeated by the game AI, self-correction in AI will be needed in the game development.

3.2   RELATED WORKS

3.2.1   AI FOR COMPUTER GAMES

AI has grown into a vital component of several games. It oversees how the game works including the behavior of non-playable characters and enemies attacking skills. It is often thought as a computer-generated mind that makes decisions, learns, and adapts to the player changing the gameplay constantly. This idea of AI is incorrect in video games (Gameranx, 2016).

Although AI is defined as the capability to obtain and understand knowledge and skills, it is not the default nature of the technology especially in the context of video games. What gets defined as AI in video games is a set of conditions created by a series of "if" statements that gets run by the computer. The actions performed by the AI are the result of the conditions being met which gives the illusion of intelligence; that the game or the entities inside the game are reacting, thinking, and learning when in reality the AI only understand the given conditions without consideration of anything else. For example, if the player is doing x, react by performing x action.

For instance, if there is an AI for an entity that has the role of patrolling a hallway, certain conditions will be given for how to react to the player. The more complex the conditions are, the more intelligent the AI will appear. This AI does not have learning capabilities that is commonly thought of. For an AI to be truly intelligent, to be capable of learning, then it has to be able to have thoughts and behaviors that have not been developed for it to do. This kind of AI is similar to human mind or cognizance simulations that are being developed by scientists however even though these simulations show signs of learning, it is not the same as human learning capabilities.

In video games, AI is developed for one purpose only, to function in certain ways that the developers have given in specific situations of the game. There are however various types of AI in video games. One type is called the rubber band AI. This AI is developed to match the skill level of the player to tailor the game experience to the player and offer more challenges by constantly observing the player's performance in the game. This is called Dynamic Game Difficulty Balancing technique. It can be used in sports games to transform the difficulty of the opposing team, or it can be used in horror and action games to change the level of enemy aggression and so forth. This use of AI increases immersion in the game.

It is not necessary for AI to be a truly learning intelligence in video games. If the video game is developed and designed with lots of detail, AI can be used as additional art that escalates the overall quality, feel, and art of the game.

Kok Wai Wonge has introduced papers that contribute to the various topics regarding the use of AI in video games as well as their current state in academia (El Rhalibi, Wong and Price, 2009). The paper "Performance simulations of moving target search algorithms" by Peter Kok Keong Loh *et al.* discusses the use of Moving Target Search (MTS) when developing bots for computer games (Loh and Prakash, 2009). MTS algorithms raise significant obstacles since they have to meet stringent specifications involving efficiency in performance and combinative computation. In this article, the authors analyze the efficiency and actions of current MTS algorithms when applied to search-and-capture gaming scenarios. As part of the study, they are also implementing a new algorithm known as MTS abstraction.

The second paper, entitled "A shortest-path lyapunov approach for forward decision processes" by Julio Clempner, is discussed where the author presents a comprehensive model for the representation of the problem of the shortest-path decision process (Clempner, 2009). Consideration is given to dynamic systems controlled by normal calculations of difference represented by Petri nets. The paper explains that by using a discrete Lyapunov-like function, the path over the net is measured forward. For the deterministic shortest path problem, natural assumptions of the default results are proven. In this context, the authors adjust the conventional cost function into a trajectory-tracking function, which is also an efficient cost-to-target network tracking function. This significantly contributes to the conceptual framework of the problem domain. The Lyapunov method presents a new principle of balance and consistency to the shortest path decision-making process.

Coleman Ron, in his paper titled "Fractal study of stealthy pathfinding aesthetics" uses a fractal framework to examine aesthetic qualities for a new category of stealth-based pathfinding that seeks to prevent detection in video games (Coleman, 2009). This study is interesting because the research on AI has provided comparatively limited attention to aesthetic findings in pathfinding. As per the fractal framework, the data published indicates that stealthy paths are distinct in their aesthetic value in comparison to control path. The author also demonstrates that paths created by various stealth rules are also unique according to statistical results.

Frank Dignum *et al.* discusses the research on multiagent systems and their potential promises in developing cognitively intelligent NPC. However, due to compatibility differences and issues, the technology is not easily implemented in game engines (Dignum *et al.*, 2009). Game engines have dynamic and instantaneous features which contribute to an increase in centralized control and efficiency, however multiagent platforms focus on the independence of agents. The use of multiagent systems to create a more independence and intelligence will help advance and improve gameplay.

In a paper titled A multiagent potential fields-based bot for real-time strategy games, Johan Hagelback *et al.* discusses the use of AI in real-time strategy games where bots are given field-based systems that allows them to plan attacks, find enemies, avoid finding each other, and explore their environment (Hagelbäck and Johansson, 2009).

A paper titled "Combining artificial intelligence methods for learning bots in a real time strategy game," written by Robin Baumgarten *et al.*, discusses how AI is used in strategy games to simulate human centric gameplay that can plan attacks and movement according to decision tree base learning, case-based reasoning (CBR), and annealing (Baumgarten, Colton and Morris, 2009).

Fabio Aiolli *et al.* in their paper titled "Enhancing artificial intelligence on a real mobile game" discusses the technical issues that encountered during game development such as creating a complex and engaging AI to play against. However, such complexity is difficult for mobile game development (Palazzi and Aiolli, 2009). The author suggests the use of a ML algorithm that solves this issue by adapting and predicting human strategies within the game.

In the paper "Breeding terrains with genetic terrain programming—the evolution of terrain generators," by Miguel Frade *et al.* discusses the role of AI in generating terrains for level design. This allows level designers to create more diverse and advanced terrain types with better features and aesthetics (Frade, Fernandez De Vega and Cotta, 2009). The paper conducted a study on the various terrains created by AI, their characteristics, and resolution. The results have shown that the use of AI in terrain generation can reserve detailed features without compromising on resolution.

"Fine-tuning parameters for emergent environments in games using artificial intelligence" by Vishnu Kotrajaras *et al*. discusses a tool for adjusting properties of developing environmental maps according to a specific situation (Kotrajaras and Kumnoonsate, 2009). The paper shows that using AI reduces time consuming and intensive work.

3.2.2 AI FOR ADAPTIVE COMPUTER GAMES

In this chapter, issues and challenges that are facing AI in video games have been discussed. These challenges include difficulty in developing complex decision spaces that do not get repetitive, difficulty in engineering all the behaviors needed for the game, not enough support for game story authors who are not expert at the programming needed for the complex behaviors, difficulty in anticipating all possible situations that are likely to be happen during gameplay, including adaptive responses to player's game preferences and choices, and lack of variations in game strategies (González-Calero and Gómez-Martín, 2011).

This chapter proposes the use and development artificial intelligent techniques that allow video games to be adaptive, smart, and responsive to the player. This can be done by learning about the player's choices, strategies, and preferences during gameplay which in turn will enable the system to adapt and perform behaviors that are more complex than what the programmers and developers have planned. This will allow the player to have a more immersive and rich experience. The author describes such a system as adaptive games.

This chapter presents three approaches for developing adaptive games through the use of CBR which includes: automatic modification of actions for creating realistic characters; managing drama and game narrative and user simulation for immersive stories; and instantaneous strategy game behavioral planning.

3.2.3 AI IN VIDEO GAMES: TOWARD A UNIFIED FRAMEWORK

This chapter discusses and proposes the use of a unified conceptual framework for developing AI in video games. The authors propose this framework as an approach to interpret and conduit between human behavior and AI (Safadi, Fonteneau and Ernst, 2015). Humans are capable to draw connection and similarities between different games which allows them to relate that knowledge while playing other games through conceptualization. The authors explain that by using a unified framework that enables developers to conceptualize their video games will contribute to solving conceptual issues found in video games.

The benefits of developing such a framework will result in reducing the redundancy and increase the robustness of AI in video games through enabling the design of AI to gain independence from individual game projects and become a central engine that can be applied to various different games which can be modified by the developers. This will help game developers in spending less time and resources in creating complex AI for each individual video game and instead modify an existing system that is robust for conceptual design.

This conceptual framework however does not apply to AI used in creating story and environment in video games.

3.2.4 Narrative in Video Games

Video games are distinct from other forms of media because of their interactivity which has an impact on storytelling. The relationship between games and storytelling as well as the role of narrative on overall gameplay has formed opposing views between game developers, scholars, and game players alike which resulted in two different philosophies to emerge in the field of game studies; Narratology and Ludology (Aarseth, 2012).

Narratology views that stories are a crucial part of game design and that it enables the player to experience events and emotions more deeply than any other form of storytelling medium. They stress that game mechanics should be designed around the narrative. While Ludology views that interactivity does not coexist with story and narrative, as well as stress that more focus should be given to mechanics and gameplay (Carlquist, 2002).

Narrative architecture is the author's model that is resulted from the division between Narratology and Ludology. He argued that the debate is based on only one form of storytelling which is the classic linear method while neglecting other methods of storytelling such as modernist and postmodernist. Instead of arguing whether or not games are a form of narrative, there should be an understanding that games are a form of narrative architecture that has no power on what the player can do once in the game world but has control on how the story gets shaped according to the possible actions or choices presented (Jenkins, 2004).

The author argues that viewing games as narrative architecture instead of focusing on Narratology or Ludology, allows for using environmental storytelling or as the author named it, "Spatial design." This design model allows for increased immersion by allowing the elements in the game design to show and embed information about the narrative. The author has identified four types of spatial design or environmental storytelling.

The first is Evoked Narrative. This spatial design provides familiar elements that are well known to the player but offers a new perspective on it. An example of this can be found in the action-adventure game *American McGee's Alice* where the game developers offer a familiar environment based on the famous story of Alice's Adventures in Wonder Land but adds horror elements to it changing the narrative perspective where the player starts to doubt the sanity of the player character and immersing the player in a new world that is interesting.

The second is Enacted Narrative. This spatial design provides conflicts and goals within the game that depends on the player's movement. This design can be found in open world games such as *Skyrim* where the player can freely explore the environment and find various quests that contain elements the feed the game narrative. Some quests especially those that contain major game narrative or plot points might require the player to proceed in the game in a specific order or to finish certain quests first.

The third is Embedded Narrative. This spatial design provides distribution of narrative information across the game world in order to control the story progression inside the game as well as challenge the player into piecing together fragments of information in order to solve puzzles and construct plot points. In this model, the game world is designed to serve as a memory palace for the player.

The fourth and final spatial design is Emergent Narrative. This provides the player with an abundant source of world building to allow the player to design their own narrative. The narrative is not pre-constructed by the developers, it is designed to be chaotic similar to the real world. The author has used The *Sims* games as example where the player can make decisions to interact with other characters, have desires, and where their decisions in the game have consequences making the player immersed and engaged while maintaining freedom in their own narrative.

3.2.5 NARRATIVE GAME MECHANICS

This chapter argues that game mechanics can be the most powerful tools for telling narrative in video games. Game developers usually use well-known mechanics and storytelling techniques such as cut-scenes, environmental storytelling, and dialogues to add narrative in their games however, this limits the narrative experiences that the developers could offer to the player because these techniques only have room to show one type of storytelling to the audience. The author believes that using narrative game mechanics can effectively tell a better story in a video game (Dubbelman, 2016).

The game mechanics and rules developed by game designers have the power to affect the player's actions within the game world without completely controlling the player. This leaves room for player freedom as well as affect the way the narrative and events take place in the game. The paper mentions the importance of creating a connection between the player and the character for this leads to immersion and investment in the game narrative. This can be done by adding conflict within the character and the environment as well as choices that evoke moral dilemmas for the player. It is important that these elements all feed the narrative of the game and not be designed in isolation.

In order to create effective narrative game mechanics, game developers must find ways to have the player involved in the construction or reconstruction of the game narrative through the actions that will be designed to be performed by the player. There must be a link between the player's actions within the game world, the character's motivation in the game narrative, and the story being told in the game. Unlike traditional storytelling methods where the creator has control over the behavior of the characters within the story through mentioning these behaviors, Interactive storytelling that is supported by games has an indirect control over the characters since the player has control inside the game world through the created game mechanics.

The author supports narrative mechanics in unfolding meaningful and interactive stories in games as opposed to focusing solely on mechanics and gameplay or viewing games as a traditional form of narrative.

An article on Gamasutra explained the rise of narrative mechanics in *Indie games*. Bycer J. has defined narrative mechanics as "A mechanic or set of mechanics, which directly influence the story through player action." (Bycer, 2012). He explained further by giving three different examples based on indie games where narrative mechanics were used. The first being the use of choices that affect the gameplay completely, the second is the use of a narrator that reacts to the player's actions within the game world, and the third is having the game track the actions of the player and providing an ending that depends on the player's actions as well as explaining how those actions led to the specific ending the player got by the end of the game.

Bycer wrote that there are endless possibilities for how narrative mechanics can evolve and change gameplay to tell better stories that are more immersive and interesting. He hoped that AAA game developing companies would start implementing them in their new games and he also recommended the use of narrative mechanics that have not been developed for games yet such as changing the behavior and appearance of NPC's according to player's behavior as well as altering the player character's senses within the games based on the rate of success or failure at solving puzzles in the game.

3.2.6 INTERACTIVE NARRATIVE

Interactive narrative is a type of interactive entertainment in video games where the player can affect the story through their actions during gameplay (Riedl, 2012). Narrative in video games provide meaning and context to game events and actions, provide motivation for player's actions in game, and acts as a link to transition the player through the various events and tasks within the game. However, the player has limited control over the events of the storyline within the game and can only have a small influence through choices which allows the game to have multiple branching storylines. Branching storylines are not often developed due to technical difficulties but AI can help create interactive narrative by creating multiple storyline branches easily and efficiently.

There are two different approaches in using AI in interactive narrative; the first is emergent narrative and the second is drama management. Emergent narrative is where the AI simulates realistic and independent characters within the game, while drama management is where the AI creates and drives the storyline of the game according to the player's actions and preferences. Interactive narrative does not just give the player control over the story but also the illusion of a realistic world full of choices and possibilities for the player to explore.

3.2.7 ADVENTURE GAMES AND PUZZLE DESIGN

The genre of adventure games allows interactive storytelling in video games through the use of puzzles and detailed game worlds. There are various sub-genres in adventure games that get classified according to the gameplay as well as themes. They follow the same steps where the player controls a character and follows a quest which requires solving puzzles to proceed with the game. Usually, the puzzles have one solution only (Afram, 2013).

There are many different puzzles in adventure games. Mostly they are about unlocking barriers such as doors or containers such as boxes. However, no matter which form the puzzle takes, it is always about coming up with a solution to remove an obstacle. There are inventory-based puzzles which requires the player to collect items and combine them. There are environmental based puzzles which requires the player to examine the environment and solve problems by interacting with it. Finally, there are puzzles that are based on NPC dialogue which requires players to solve problems by having dialogues with the NPCs.

Puzzles in video games have a strong impact where they can affect the player's actions and progress the story. They give meaning to in-game actions such as inspecting items to find clues and search for a solution. They can also have consequences by giving punishments or rewards that affects the overall story and progression. Puzzles must be designed to allow the player to progress in the story and game goals where they are will not be perceived as meaningless obstacles but meaningful and impactful choices that makes the game progress.

The thesis discusses ten principles for designing puzzles in video games. The first is to make them easy to understand so that the players do not feel confused. The second is to make them easy to begin solving them so that the players do not feel intimidated and try to solve them. The third is showing progress where the player can feel that they are accomplishing something by interacting and manipulating the objects available. The fourth is to show that the puzzle can be solved by giving the player cues of progress. The fifth is making the puzzle interesting by adding more difficult challenges. The sixth is giving the player multiple options to progress the game. Scattering different puzzles that the player can choose from to avoid frustration resulted from lack of progression. The seventh is to show the player that all elements of the puzzles are connected which helps solve more difficult challenges. The eighth is to offer clues that can help the player in solving the puzzle. The ninth is showing the answer to the puzzle indirectly so that when the player finds the solution, they gain a sense of accomplishment. The final principle is to be careful of using optical illusions in puzzle design which might make the player feel frustrated.

3.2.8　The Horror Genre and Video Games

This book section discusses how the Horror genre is one of the most ideal genres to be adapted and used in video games going back to the genre's roots which can be traced back to the text interactive game Zork created in 1980. This game marked the beginning of the shift from Adventure games to Horror by introducing the concept of death to the player for the first time. The Horror genre started to evolve and become more popular with many games being introduced in the market such as *Mystery House, Maniac Mansion, Silent Hill,* and many others that followed (Rouse, 2009).

Video games will always have constraints in creating a realistic world. This, however, is one of the reasons why Horror games are one of the ideal genres for video games because although Horror games take place in a familiar place that should be realistic, it is designed with the purpose of making it seem different and out of the ordinary while offering the player justification for the strange environment, abilities, and events. The familiar environment also grounds the player and makes the experience more interesting unlike fantasy and science fiction games, where the unique characteristics of the game is a result of a foreign world.

The author argues that the video games and the Horror genre share overlapping goals which has been a driving reason for the success of the genre as well as one of the reasons why Horror games have potential to grow and evolve.

The Horror genre is one of the most popular video game genres with the youth (Krzywinska, 2002). It is a unique genre because unlike movies and books, it makes the player feels scared and immersed in the environment due to its interactivity.

Horror helps young adults confront and master their fears in a safe space (Jamie Madigan, 2015). This helps releasing feelings of anxiety caused by real world fears and worries and replacing it with feelings of relief and exhilaration as well as a sense of reward from conquering their own fear (Elio Martino, 2019).

Experiencing fear in a fictional environment causes a rush of emotions that other video game genres are unable to provide. This is a result of the excitation transfer theory where fear transfers feelings of pleasure similar to that of riding a roller coaster knowing that it is safe (Nicolas Brown, 2020).

This article discusses the various issues modern Horror games face and how they are different to older games of the same genre. The author argues that horror games have fallen out of fashion and are no longer popular in the game industry. AAA game development companies have moved away from the genre despite the enormous successes of games such as *Dead Space 3* and *Resident Evil 6*. This is due to the industry's focus on combat which has resulted in the rise of Action-Horror games rather than focusing on puzzle-solving, narrative, and adventure.

Meanwhile, the independent game development companies such as Frictional Games, started to stay away from action-horror and implement new game mechanics (such as stealth and sanity) to help the player focus on story while also increasing fear elements in the game. The success of the game has resulted in a popularity with indie horror games with many games being released in the market using similar mechanics of stealth as well as removing combat (Bycer, 2019).

However, many of these games lack an understanding of psychology behind what evokes tension and fear in the player as well as what immerses the player into the world and the narrative of the game. This includes providing the player with details about the game world and narrative as well as game mechanic and loops that keeps the player immersed in the story. The difficulties of designing these elements are one of the reasons that independent game developers have switched to a different approach; designing games for an audience instead of players. With a rise of a trend called "Let's Play" has started gaining popularity on YouTube in 2010. With many YouTubers creating videos of themselves playing and reacting to these games.

This article is significant to the proposed project because it explains the current issues in Modern Horror game design and shows how they are different from the classic Horror games.

In this chapter, a tool has been designed to help game developers in creating a horror game. The author points out the difficulty in developing horror games due to the different interpretation the nature of fear. This chapter offers a solution by categorizing fear on a scale tool that measures the level of fear in game events. This tool helps the developer in understanding how certain game mechanics, lighting, and enemy design should be like in order to achieve the desired emotional response from the player as well as plan the intensity of certain game events along with the pacing. The tool also acts as a bridge between understanding the psychology behind fear and enjoyment in horror video games (Ntokos, 2018).

It is crucial to understand the emotions that are desired to be provoked in the player and understand how these emotions contribute to the player's enjoyment and immersion. The level of fear tool contains ten levels of fear which explain the intensity of the emotion.

The author advices game developer to use the scale shown in Table 3.1 to plan the game events and develop accordingly. The scale tool can be applied to be used on atmosphere, audio, and Enemy AI.

Atmosphere is crucial in horror games where it controls the player's feel in the environment. Atmosphere is the element that sets the feel, style, and tone in the environment. It contains elements such as sound, lighting, and gameplay experience. Darkness is suitable for creating a scary atmosphere for the player where the darkness pushes the player to imagine their surroundings and increase tension. Any element that blocks player's visibility will create a sense of unease.

Audio has a strong impact on player experience and game atmosphere. In Horror games, Auditory Hallucinations affect the player's experience by increasing tension and fear through hearing sounds that did not happen (Demarque and

TABLE 3.1
Levels of Fear (see Ntokos, 2018)

Level	Emotion	Meaning	Example
1	Calmness	Peaceful state of mind. No fear.	Beginning of the game where the player is exploring the environment and learning the mechanics. It could also be used in safe rooms or guarded areas.
2	Nervousness	Player gains information of strange knowledge that causes interest and doubts.	Non-direct events that the player hears or reads about without enough explanation.
3	Vigilance	Player starts to feel fear and pays attention to the surroundings.	Direct evidence of the strange events the player encountered before.
4	Restlessness	The player's fear starts to hinder level exploration.	Sound effects and strange changes in the environment.
5	Tense	Player feels fear from any minor change in the environment without direct evidence.	Hearing voices, sounds in the environment like doors and wood creaking.
6	Distress	Players starts to have survival instincts instead of thinking clearly.	Witness a distressing event through visuals or audio cues.
7	Fright	Players starts to have quick reflexes as a reaction to the survival instincts.	An enemy getting nearby and the events of subtle Jump scares.
8	Dread	The player's fear and survival instincts cause immersion and focus in the game to avoid getting detected by the enemy.	An enemy patrolling near the player.
9	Panic	The player must make quick actions to survive.	Combat, enemy chase, managing resources to survive.
10	Terror	Player losses control to fight or flight instinct. Player might jump out of the seat or scream.	Player death, near death by an enemy, surprise attack.

Relief and enjoyment due to rush of adrenalin

Lima, 2013). They have various types and forms such as strange noises of ghosts or crying.

This chapter conducted an experiment where people got to play two different versions of the same game. One has Auditory Hallucination and one without. The results have shown that people who played the game with Auditory Hallucination felt more scared playing the game.

The Survival Horror genre has many elements that makes it perfect for storytelling and narration and trying to understand the genre from the narrative perspective helps shed light to many aspects in Horror games that makes it unique from other genres as well as better at implementing effective narrative structures in the game. The player character is always put in situations where (s)he takes the role of a detective who is exploring and investigating their surrounding environment. This makes the player engaged in the game and trying to reconstruct the narrative of the game while also being unsure about the strange and paranormal elements happening in the game world and threatening the character. The player's goal is not just to discover the story, but to find a solution and escape at the same time. This structure is one of the reasons that characters in Horror games usually suffer from memory loss. This enables the player to share the experience of uncovering the past with the character creating a connection and increasing immersion.

Environmental storytelling is one of the powerful mechanics used in horror games where narrative is being unfolded to the player through the game world and architecture. The buildings, objects such as toys, furniture, or notes are used to tell stories from the past. The level design becomes a crucial part of the game narrative and almost treated as one of the characters in the game (Kirkland, 2009).

Survival Horror games show that there are ways to represent narrative in an interactive game experience through spatial environmental design even though the player's pathway is designed in the game world through quests and tasks. Storytelling in Survival Horror is also designed to feed the player the sense of not being in control in an interactive narrative experience. However, in order to achieve this, storytelling usually takes a linear design in the game giving the player the illusion of being in control over the story events while providing the player with interactivity. This causes a sense of fear and tension in the game through showing that there are more powerful dark forces that control the narrative and manipulate the player in the game world.

3.3 PLAYER EXPERIENCE

A framework has been presented in a paper published by Hunicke, Leblanc and Zubek (2004) that has been developed for the Game Developers Conference. The MDA framework which stands for Mechanics, Dynamics, and Aesthetics is a formal method to understand games and game design. It is also developed to link between game development, criticism, and research creating a unified and easy approach for studying and designing games that can be used by both developers and scholars alike.

Design methodologies are crucial for creating any artifact. They are the processes that guarantee the quality of a project. Using an iterative, quantitative, and qualitative methods help the game designer in analyzing both the end results to improve project implementation, and the implementation process to improve the final result. This method of approaching the project from both the viewpoints, allow various possibilities and dependencies when creating systems and subsystems in a game that need to interact with each other dynamic and complex behaviors inside the game.

The MDA framework is designed to help designers and game developers to closely examine interdependencies in a game in order to create the desired end result while scholars and researchers need to study and understand them before making any conclusions on the game experience resulted by them.

Players view the game as a set of rules which need to be followed, these rules build the system that is being played and playing the system results in the player having fun. This view can be formalized using the MDA model to be used by the developers as follows; the game contains mechanics which are the basic structure of the game and the code that forms the rules, Dynamics are the result of the interdependencies of the mechanics, how they affect the player's input and the game's output to the player, and finally the Aesthetics are the player's emotional responses and experiences in the game.

This framework is built on a fundamental idea that video games should be described as artifacts and not as media. The author suggests that video games identified as artifacts mean that the behavior of a game is formed by its content and their interactions together forming a system and not the media elements that are presented to the player.

Each element of the MDA framework can be used to view separate parts of the game that can be linked together to provide the full experience desired by the developers as shown in Figure 3.1. The designer views the mechanics as the elements that creates the dynamic behaviors in the system, these dynamics create the desired aesthetic experiences to the player. However, the player views the aesthetics as the main element that sets the mood of the game which is a result of the dynamics and lastly, the underlying mechanics.

The author urges developers and researchers to think about both the views of the designer and the player in order to understand how game elements interdepend and interact with one another as well as create a game that focuses on player experience as opposed to a game that focuses on the given features and mechanics.

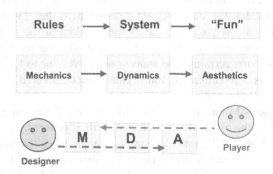

FIGURE 3.1   The MDA framework (see Hunicke, Leblanc and Zubek, 2004).

In a thesis done by Tanskanen (2018), on the effects of immersion on player experience explains that immersion is created from different parts; the first is narrative which contains the story and plot in the game. The second is spatial which includes the player exploring the environment. The third is effective which includes the player's emotional involvement in the game. The fourth is shared which is about the interaction between the various elements of the game. The fifth is kinesthetic which includes controlling the player character, and finally the sixth and last is ludic which includes players in game choices and their consequences.

The thesis explains how narrative and spatial involvement the biggest impact on player immersion can have where the player moves in the environment and interacts with the narrative forming emotional involvement. This is why the author suggested the importance of creating a detailed document for the game environment in order to plan and list the aspects of immersion to make the game believable and immersive.

In a paper by Boonen and Mieritz (2018), methods for manipulating the player's agency in horror games have been discussed. Agency is defined as the player's reaction when a wanted action is supported by the game. The paper has designed a model for Agency that explains the relationships between the various elements that can be used to manipulate the player's agency. Those are parameters of player character which contain the aspects that concern the player character, the second is parameters of system which contains the aspects of game and game world limitations, parameters of player.

The parameters of player character contain two sub-parameters; the first is physical parameters which are the physical limitations of the player character. And the second is psychological parameters which are the limitations of the player character's psyche such as having a sanity system.

The parameters of the system also contain two sub-parameters; the first is about the obstacles in the environment such as enemies, building, and resources. The second is about the limitations created by game mechanics such as locks. Finally, the parameters of the player are about the limitations and skills of the player in the game.

It is crucial to plan and consider the movement of the player character within the environment as well as the space and placement of the objects within it. The level design should be realistic following the rules of physics. This is important to consider because it plays a role in player immersion.

There are two different types of level structures; linear and non-linear. Linear level design is suitable for story-focused games where the player must follow a certain path to reveal the plot. This limits the freedom of the player withing the level. Meanwhile, non-linear level design is flexible allowing the player freedom to explore without locking certain game areas or objectives due to following a specific story. However, it is argued that non-linear games are considered linear because the player's movement is planned.

A research done by Milam and El Nasr (2010) in the different types in level design and how they affect the player character based on their patterns. The paper discuses five different push and pull game mechanics as approaches for game designers to control and manipulate players movement in the game environment.

The first pattern is path of movement and resistance which is used with narrative purposes in game such as player objectives which sets the player on a path to reach a certain goal while resistance is the challenges that stand in front of the player blocking the player from achieving their objectives. This kind of pattern leads the player to find a solution to remove the resistance and continue with the objective.

The second pattern is based on AI movement where the player moves in the environment responding to the movements and actions of AI characters in game which can be NPCs or enemies.

The third pattern is based on a target path where the player needs to reach a certain visible target which directs and moves the character to that location.

The fourth pattern is based on collection paths where the player moves in the environment motivated by collecting rewards or resources such as battery pickups or coins.

The fifth and final pattern is player vulnerability path which forces the player to adapt to the environment due to vulnerability in a given scenario such as needing to hide to avoid enemies.

3.4   METHODOLOGIES USED IN GAME DEVELOPMENT

The Agile methodology is one of the most simple and efficient methods that a developer can rely on to design and develop a software. It is a method that uses continuous planning, learning, collaboration, and improvement to deliver early and offer flexibility for changes due to client requirements or emerging new technologies.

The Agile methodology focuses on how projects should be worked on differently depending on their type and needs. It combines both iterative and incremental processes with a focus on having a highly adaptive approach and focus on client satisfaction through rapid development. It breaks down the project tasks into incremental parts or time boxes that are developed in a series of short iterations. The project is not designed in one sequential order from beginning to end, but developing small features and functionalities in small time periods. Each iteration is like a mini version of the project where the results are used to review and adjust the project plan.

These iterations are like a short time frame where every iteration lasts around one to four weeks. Each iteration goes through the project life cycle including planning, requirements gathering, design, coding, and testing. They include certain features in the project where a working product is shown to the client by the end of each iteration and at the last iteration, the final project includes all the features and requirements that were defined at the start of the development process.

The initial requirements and scope of the research is decided and defined by the start of the development phase including the number of needed iterations and the overall duration of the project which avoids the risk of scope creep. The Agile methodology also focuses on developing a project in a swift manner through iterations and increments which helps reduce the risk in the project as well as reducing the time for working on tasks and requirements before a functional product is shown to the client.

A functional prototype has been designed and implemented inside Unreal Engine using Unreal Engine Blueprints in a duration of four weeks. During this time, various

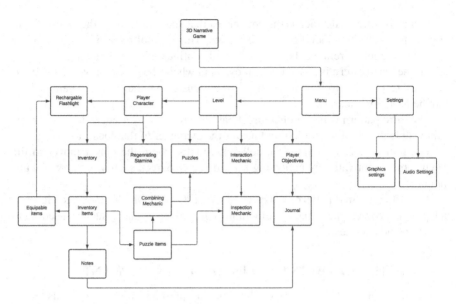

FIGURE 3.2   Proposed functionality diagram.

games have been observed to gather references and understand their requirements and functionalities until initial features for the proposed project have been identified. Various sources and tutorials have been studied to learn how to implement the initial identified features inside Unreal Engine as shown in Figure 3.2.

Game development projects share many similarities with software engineering projects (Kortmann and Harteveld, 2009). Agile methodologies are suitable for complex projects where requirements needed are not clear at the start of the project. Game development projects are complex with uncertain requirements that might need to change during development due to its multidisciplinary nature where various skills and tasks are needed from art design, sound, gameplay, and programming (Petrillo and Pimenta, 2010). This causes difficulties for clients to have a clear picture of the needed outcomes at the start of project development. Agile methodology allows developers to gain better understanding to the needs of the clients as well as provide suitable solutions to improve the quality of the project as well as add efficiency in development by spending more time adding improvements to the project. Therefore, many game developments companies have applied the use of Agile methodologies (Stacey and Nandhakumar, 2008).

The functional prototype is implemented in the third person design template of Unreal Engine. This template includes a third person character and camera where the camera follows the player character in the three-dimensional (3D) space as shown in Figure 3.3. The first-person mode has been designed by moving the camera to the head of the player and linking it to the head mesh so that it moves with the movement of the player character. A spotlight has been added in front of the head mesh to create the light for the flashlight. The arrow attached to the character mesh points at the direction which the player character faces when spawned in the level.

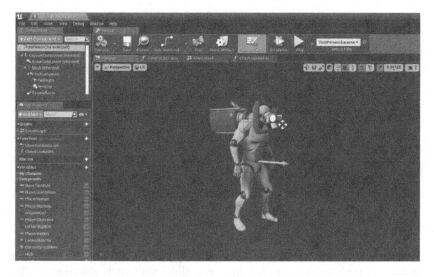

FIGURE 3.3   Player character class in UE4.

The player can walk and look around in all directions inside the 3D space by using the mouse and keyboard to navigate in the *x*, *y*, and *z* axes. When the player presses the w, s, a, and d keyboard buttons, the coordinate in the background gets updated accordingly.

Screenshot of the player's screen in the functional prototype. The player has a user interface where it shows the player's hunger and stamina levels. These bars decrease by time where hunger can get regenerated through picking up consumable items (minor food pickup and full food pickup), the stamina gets regenerated by time however the player character will not be able to sprint as long as the stamina is getting regenerating.

In the bottom, there is the flashlight battery that shows the player how much battery is left as shown in Figures 3.4, 3.5 and 3.6. The player will not be able to turn on the flashlight if the battery is empty and must pick up batteries to refill.

FIGURE 3.4   First person game view.

FIGURE 3.5   Inspect item prompt.

There is an objectives icon that is dynamic meaning it changes and get updated according to the player's actions. If the player collides with a new objective, it will be added and shown on the UI. If the player completes an objective, objective complete message will be shown.

The screenshot shows the use of the interaction and inspection system in the prototype. This is implemented by creating a Line Trace that reads if there are any inspectable items for the player to pick. A message is shows to the player if the player is looking at an inspectable item.

Items are created as child to a parent item having similar main characteristics including being picked up and inspected by the player. In the screenshot, the player is looking at the parent item where a message shows the player that (s)he can inspect the item.

The player picks up the inspectable item where a message is shown explaining that using left click allows item inspection while right click drops the item on the floor being impacted by physics.

When the player left clicks to inspect the item, (s)he can rotate the item by left clicking and moving the mouse. There is also an option to zoom by scrolling the

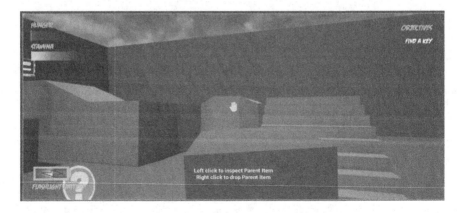

FIGURE 3.6   Player picks item.

FIGURE 3.7   Item inspection.

mouse well. Item description can be visible on the side. The description is dynamic and changes according to the item being held. This is scripted inside the script graph of the inspection UI. The player can exit inspection mode by right clicking twice; first to hold the item and second time to drop the item.

The design of the user interface has been designed inside Unreal Engine widgets as shown in Figure 3.8.

Figure 3.6 shows the blueprints for an AI going toward the player. This is done by creating a trigger box and placing it in the scene at the desired location. A trigger box is a box collision that is invisible to the player in game. It is used to trigger events when something overlaps with it. In Figure 3.7, the box is triggered by the player character by casting or calling the player's class and from this class, the location of the player is stored in the blueprint and used to for playing a sound effect. This is done by getting a play sound at location node and connecting the player's location

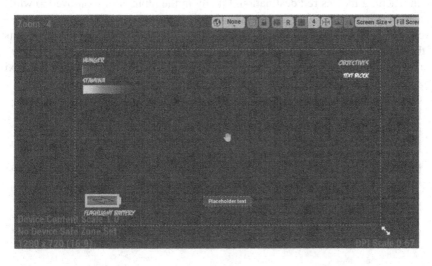

FIGURE 3.8   User interface.

FIGURE 3.9   Main menu.

to the location input of the node. Then the AI actor is stored in the blueprint by getting all the actors from the AI class. This enables the developer to access any actor
in the specified class as shown in Figures 3.9 and 3.10. The actors are then stored
as a copy and the AI actor set to visible. An AI move to node is added. This node
enables the AI to move toward the desired location. The pawn is connected to the
object reference, specifying which actor or which AI should be moved. The location
input is a vector variable representing the desired destination the AI should move to.
The target actor input is also an object or actor reference however, this input is for
specifying an actor whom the AI is targeted to move toward. Acceptance radius is
a float variable that specifies the value on which the success of the event is based on
upon reaching the desired destination. Finally in the input is stop on overlap which
is a Boolean variable that specifies whether or not the AI will stop moving when
overlapping or colliding with something. In the output there are three different exits;
if the first is connected, then any nodes or events that follow will happen no matter if
the AI move node succeeded in going to the desired location or not. The second exit

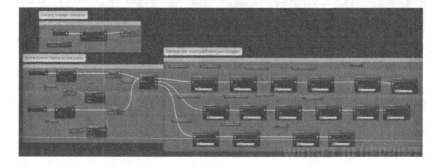

FIGURE 3.10   Journal blueprint.

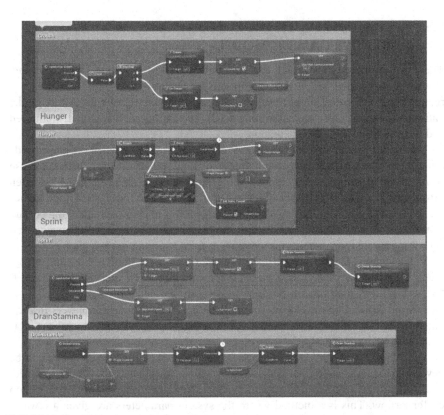

FIGURE 3.11   Player hunger and stamina.

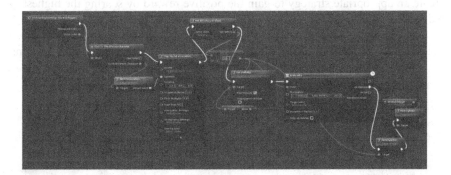

FIGURE 3.12   Blueprint of AI based functionality.

is for the success of the node, and the third is for the failure. Finally in the output is the movement result which stores the result of the path followed for later use.

After the success of the AI move node, the AI actor is destroyed as well as the trigger box to ensure that the player does not trigger the event again and avoid any bugs. Overall blueprint of the game is shown in Figures 3.11 and 3.12.

3.5   AI ELEMENTS IN THE PROPOSED
NARRATIVE GAMING MODEL

There are multiple types of ML algorithms that could be applied for the gaming. However, supervised ML is not appropriate for narrative gaming. Therefore, it is recommended to either adopt unsupervised or reinforced algorithms. Although the gaming is done in controlled environment, but the patterns are being read, monitored and recorded for the pattern detection.

This pattern paves way for the next set of player experience when the player finds a totally new experience based on its previous input pattern (Comi, 2018). The use of AI in video games is not compatible despite the widespread belief. AI is often mistaken for artificial behavior of agents in a video game. Agents in video games are required to offer enough engagement for the player to enjoy a challenging but fun experience. Agents should not outsmart the player resulting in a frustrating experience, but imitate human behavior in having weaknesses and imperfections.

Video games can be viewed as more than just a medium of fun and enjoyment, they can be viewed as a medium for studying and experimenting the different developments that can be done in a variety of fields related to AI. Google DeepMind worked on developing an agent capable of outsmarting players in their game *AlphaGo* which led to beating the best Go player and score a goal that was not considered possible.

The article written by Comi discusses how an artificial intelligent agent can be developed to play a game such as the "Snake" game. To achieve this, Comi explained, a deep reinforcement learning algorithm should be implemented using Keras on top of Tensorflow. This is a method where the system parameters are given a reward; either positive or negative, based on its actions. The agent is not given any information about the game rules, leaving it to figure out what needs to be done by itself and create an appropriate strategy to gain the positive reward by scoring the highest in the game.

In this way, a video game can show how an AI agent with the help of Deep Q-learning, can learn to play the game *snake*, and come up with suitable gaming

FIGURE 3.13   Overview of the scene.

FIGURE 3.14 User interface of game design platform – Unreal Engine.

strategies in order to gain the highest scores. The author has conducted study where a Deep Q-learning algorithm has scored 50 points after just five minutes of training on playing the game *Snake*. The *Snake* game was developed using Python and Pygame, which is a library that allows developers to create simple games using Python. At first the AI agent did not know how to play the game as it was not trained yet, however, after 100 iterations which is equivalent to five minutes of playing, the agent started to score points and after 200 iterations, the agent scored 83 points.

The method of reinforcement learning is based on the Markov Decision Process. This process provides a mathematical framework that creates random decision-making outcomes. The author has used Deep Q-learning instead of ML because in ML, the agent is trained with a targeted input and output. The output is the correct answer where they are required to be predicted according to the inputs provided. This method is not effective because it does not show which action is the best to be taken in the game to score the highest score.

When using reinforcement learning, two components are present, those are, the game which represents the environment and the snake which represents the AI agent that has the deep neural network creating the decisions of the snake in game. When the agents performs and action, a positive or negative reward is then provided by the environment which depends on how that specific action taken by the agent was beneficial to that game state. The agent then has an objective to learn the best strategy of actions that provide the best rewards in each game state. The game state is the observations received by the agent throughout different iterations in the game environment. It can vary between variables such as position and speed. The agent's decision-making process to determine the best strategy of actions in the game is called a policy according to the reinforcement learning method.

The AI agent makes decisions according to the Q-table which is a matrix that shows the association between all the possible actions that can be taken by the agent according to its state in the environment. Values are given in the table according to the probability of each action's success and their rewards. However, the author argues that there is a problem with the policy in reinforcement learning because it is represented in a table. This constrains the space for the states in the environment and makes it difficult to have a large number of different states. Therefore, using Deep Q-learning is preferred because it represents the policy in a deep neural network where the values are changed by applying the Bellman equation.

The algorithm for the snake agent is explained as follows: Firstly, the game starts and a Q-value is given randomly. Secondly, the state is recognized by the system. Thirdly, an action is taken according to the recognized state. The action taken can be random at first to allow exploration and maximize learning so that later the agent can depend on its neural network. Finally, the agent gets rewarded from the environment according to the action taken and how it affects the current state. Then the Q-value is updated by using the Bellman equation which results in generating a new state accordingly. The data of the original state, action, reward, and the updated states are all stored to be used in training the neural network in a method called Replay Memory. The operations repeat until the game ends or another condition is met.

A state is explained as representing the agent's situation as well as the neural network input. In the study done by the author, an array of eleven Boolean variables was given for the states in the snake game. Those states contained Booleans for whether or not the agent is close to danger, the direction of the agent's movement, and the position of food.

The agent should try to get the maximum number of positive rewards and get the minimum number of negative rewards. In the snake game, positive rewards are given by adding ten points to the score every time the snake (AI agent) eats a fruit, while negative rewards are given by removing 10 points from the score every time the snake (AI agent) hits itself or a wall. Additional points can be added to the score when for each move the snake takes while avoiding death, this affects the decision-making process for the AI were moving in a in a certain way can get additional rewards. This shows that by applying reinforced learning, an AI can outsmart the human players by using flaws in opponents' strategies to come up with action that are unanticipated.

The study done by the author shows that a simple AI agent can learn how to understand the mechanics of an environment, create decisions to gain positive rewards and avoid negative rewards without being informed of the rules, and respond in unanticipated way by using flaws in opponents' strategies.

3.6   Q-ALGORITHM FOR AI IN GAMING

Using Q-algorithm for reinforcement learning for AI has various advantages such as being simple and flexible to use. Q-learning is divided into two stages: one for training and the other for exploitation. In the training stage, the AI agent explores the environment at random and storing values in the Q-table of all the positive and negative rewards it has received during exploration. These values are later used to predict which actions would be beneficial to get positive rewards and which actions would

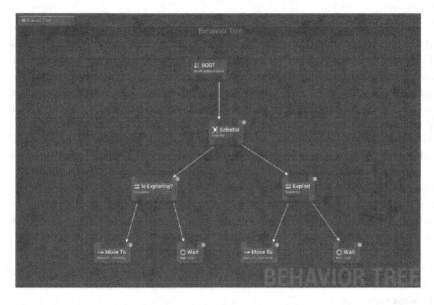

FIGURE 3.15   AI behavior tree for the two stages of Q-learning.

lead to negative rewards or no rewards at all in the future. This process is the process behind the AI agent decision making during the second stage which is exploitation (sacredgames, 2017).

The author has given the equation below for *Q*-learning:

$$Q(\text{state, action}) = R(\text{state, action}) + \text{Gamma} * \text{Max}\left[Q(\text{next state, all actions})\right]$$

An example has been done in Unreal Engine to show the use of Q-learning on an AI agent where the agent or none player character starts the training stage by moving at random between four locations in the environment. The four locations include three bowls containing food and a switch. Each location has their own values associated to them and the AI agent learns their values as well as associated behavior (how to get food from the bowls and how the light switch can affect the availability of food) during the training stage.

The desired outcome is for the agent to start making decisions and behave with intention according to the values and behaviors found and observed during the training stage. The agent should be able to identify that food can be obtained from the three bowls only if the light switch is turned on therefore the AI agent is expected to be able to go to the light switch first then go to the food bowls.

Q learning algorithm provides an AI agent with realistic lifelike and dynamic behavior by imitating the drive behind the carrot and stick example. The agent's decisions are based on the rewards available in the environment which is stored in a table containing all the possible rewards both positive and negative. It can be used for creating various intentional behaviors to enhance gameplay by having more lifelike non player characters.

3.7 CONCLUSION

AI has become an integral part in game development. This chapter focuses the use of AI in 3D narrative games for enhancing the player's experience and increasing immersion. This is proposed by using AI or ML to create immersive, complex, and dynamic game narratives, which changes according to the player's play-pattern and allows the player to have more freedom and make interesting choices. Various approaches have been studied in this chapter including approaches for narrative game design, enhancing the player's experience through the use of the MDA model, and the use of AI in creating dynamic video games. It has been found that there are various types of AI that is used in game development which are usually created on a rule-based system which conditions the AI to make certain behaviors as a response to different scenarios but sometimes ML is used to allow the AI to learn and adapt to the player's patterns. However, supervised ML is not appropriate for narrative games. Therefore, this study recommends the use of unsupervised or reinforced algorithms in developing narrative games. This allows the player to be in a controlled environment but also allows the AI to be able to learn and record the player's patterns and responds accordingly creating an enjoyable and immersive playing experience.

REFERENCES

Aarseth, E. (2012) 'A narrative theory of games', in *In Proceedings of the international conference on the foundations of digital games*, pp. 129–133. doi: 10.1145/2282338.2282365.

Afram, Rabi. "Puzzle Design in Adventure Games." (2013),Degree Project in Game Design, 15 ECTS Credits Game Design and Programming, Spring 2013.

Anderton Kevin (2018) *The Impact Of Gaming: A Benefit To Society [Infographic], Forbes.*

Baumgarten, R., Colton, S. and Morris, M. (2009) 'Combining AI methods for learning bots in a real-time strategy game', *International Journal of Computer Games Technology*, 2009, pp. 1–10. doi: 10.1155/2009/129075.

Boonen, C. S. and Mieritz, D. (2018) 'Paralysing fear: player agency parameters in Horror games', in *Proceedings of Nordic DiGRA 2018*.

Brown, A. D., Stacey, P., & Nandhakumar, J. (2008). Making sense of sensemaking narratives. Human Relations, 61(8), 1035–1062. doi:10.1177/0018726708094858

Butler, M. (2016) *Why People Play Horror Games, iNews.*

Bycer, J. (2012) *Extreme Storytelling: The Use of Narrative Mechanics, Gamasutra.*

Bycer, J. (2019) *The Problem of Modern Horror Game Design - Game Wisdom, Game Wisdom.*

Carlquist, J. (2002) 'Playing the Story Computer Games as a Narrative Genre', *Human IT: Journal for Information Technology Studies as a Human Science*, 6(3), pp. 7–53.

Clempner, J. B. (2009) 'A Shortest-path Lyapunov Approach for Forward Decision Processes', *International Journal of Computer Games Technology*, Volume 2009, pp. 1–12. doi: 10.1155/2009/162450.

Coleman, R. (2009) 'Fractal Analysis of Stealthy Pathfinding Aesthetics', *International Journal of Computer Games Technology*, Volume 2009, pp. 1–7. doi: 10.1155/2009/670459.

Comi, M. (2018) 'How to Teach AI to Play Games: Deep Reinforcement Learning', Towards Data Science. Available at: https://towardsdatascience.com/how-to-teach-an-ai-to-play-games-deep-reinforcement-learning-28f9b920440a (Accessed: 7 March 2021).

Demarque, T. C. and Lima, E. S. De (2013) 'Auditory Hallucination: Audiological Perspective for Horror Games', *Sbgames.Org*, Volume 2013, pp. 19–26.

Dignum, F. *et al.* (2009) 'Games and Agents: Designing Intelligent Gameplay', *International Journal of Computer Games Technology*, Volume 2009, pp. 1–18. doi: 10.1155/2009/837095.

Dubbelman, T. (2016) 'Narrative game mechanics', in *International Conference on Interactive Digital Storytelling*. Springer Verlag, pp. 39–50. doi: 10.1007/978-3-319-48279-8_4.

Elio Martino (2019) Why We Love Survival Horror, Psychology Today.

Ferguson, C. J., & Colwell, J. (2020). Sexualised video games, sexist attitudes and empathy towards victims of rape: Correlational evidence for a relationship is minimal in an online study. Criminal Behaviour and Mental Health. doi:10.1002/cbm.2138

Frade, M., Fernandez De Vega, F. and Cotta, C. (2009) 'Breeding Terrains with Genetic Terrain Programming: The Evolution of Terrain Generators', *International Journal of Computer Games Technology*, Volume 2009, pp. 1–13. doi: 10.1155/2009/125714.

Gameranx (2016) How Does Video Game AI Work?, YouTube.

González-Calero, P. A. and Gómez-Martín, M. A. (2011) 'Artificial Intelligence for Computer Games', *Artificial Intelligence for Computer Games*, (Ccl), pp. 1–200. doi: 10.1007/978-1-4419-8188-2.

Hagelbäck, J. and Johansson, S. J. (2009) 'A Multiagent Potential Field-Based Bot for Real-Time Strategy Games', *International Journal of Computer Games Technology*, Volume 2009, pp. 1–10. doi: 10.1155/2009/910819.

Hunicke, R., Leblanc, M. and Zubek, R. (2004) 'MDA: A formal Approach to Game Design and Game Research', *AAAI Workshop - Technical Report*, WS-04-04, pp. 1–5.

Madigan, J. (2015) *The Psychology of Horror Games*, The Psychology of Video Games.

Jenkins, H. (2004) 'Game Design as Narrative Architecture', in Harrigan, P. and Wardrip-Fruin, N. (eds.) *First Person: New Media As Story, Performance, and Game*. US, Cambridge, pp. 118–129.

Kirkland, E. (2009) 'Storytelling in survival horror video games', in Perron, B. (ed.) *Horror Video Games: Essays on the Fusion of Fear and Play*. Jefferson, North Carolina: McFarland & Company, Inc., pp. 62–78.

Kortmann, Rens & Harteveld, Casper. (2009). Agile game development: Lessons learned from software engineering.

Kotrajaras, V. and Kumnoonsate, T. (2009) 'Fine-Tuning Parameters for Emergent Environments in Games Using Artificial Intelligence', *International Journal of Computer Games Technology*, Volume 2009, pp. 1–9. doi: 10.1155/2009/436732.

Krzywinska, T. (2002) 'Hands-On Horror', *ScreenPlay. Cinema/Videogames/Interfaces.*, 2(Fall), pp. 12–23.

Loh, P. K. K. and Prakash, E. C. (2009) 'Performance Simulations of Moving Target Search Algorithms', *International Journal of Computer Games Technology*, Volume 2009, pp. 1–6. doi: 10.1155/2009/745219.

Milam, D. and El Nasr, M. S. (2010) 'Design patterns to guide player movement in 3D games', in *Proceedings - Sandbox 2010: 5th ACM SIGGRAPH Symposium on Video Games*, pp. 37–41. doi: 10.1145/1836135.1836141.

Nicolas Brown (2020) Why Do We Enjoy Horror Games?, TechRaptor.

Ntokos, K. (2018) '"Level of Fear": Analysis of Fear Spectrum into a Tool to Support Horror Game Design for Immersion and Fear', *An International Journal (CGDEIJ)*, 1(1), pp. 33–43.

Palazzi, C. E. and Aiolli, F. (2009) 'Enhancing Artificial Intelligence on a Real Mobile Game', *International Journal of Computer Games Technology*, Volume 2009, pp. 1–9. doi: 10.1155/2009/456169.

Petrillo, F., & Pimenta, M. (2010). Is agility out there? Proceedings of the 28th ACM International Conference on Design of Communication - SIGDOC '10. doi:10.1145/1878450.1878453.

El Rhalibi, A., Wong, K. W. and Price, M. (2009) 'Artificial intelligence for computer games', *International Journal of Computer Games Technology*, Volume 2009, pp. 1–3. doi: 10.1155/2009/251652.

Riedl, M. O. (2012) 'Interactive Narrative: A Novel Application of Artificial Intelligence for Computer Games Artificial Intelligence in Computer Games', in *Proceedings of the Twenty-Sixth AAAI Conference on Artificial Intelligence*. Atlanta, Georgia, USA: Georgia Institute of Technology, pp. 2160, 2165.

Rouse, R. (2009) 'Match Made in Hell: The Inevitable Success of the Horror Genre in Video Games', in Perron, B. (ed.) *Horror Video Games Essays on the Fusion of Fear and Play*. Jefferson, North Carolina: McFarland & Company, Inc., pp. 15–25.

sacredgames, (2017) "Reinforcement Learning: Q-Algorithm in a Match to Sample Task – Machine Learning In Unreal Engine," *sacredgames*, December 19. https://unrealai.wordpress.com/2017/12/19/q-learning/ (accessed Mar. 16, 2021)

Safadi, F., Fonteneau, R. and Ernst, D. (2015) 'Artificial Intelligence in Video Games: Towards a Unified Framework', *International Journal of Computer Games Technology*, 2015, pp. 1–30. doi: 10.1155/2015/271296.

Sikali, K. (2020) 'The Dangers of Social Distancing: How COVID-19 can Reshape our Social Experience', *Journal of Community Psychology*, 48(8), pp. 2435–2438. doi: 10.1002/jcop.22430.

Tanskanen, S. (2018) 'Player Immersion in Video Games Designing an Immersive Game Project', p. 75.

4 Review on Using Artificial Intelligence Related Deep Learning Techniques in Gaming and Recent Networks

Mujahid Tabassum, Sundresan Perumal,
Hadi Nabipour Afrouzi, Saad Bin Abdul
Kashem, and Waqar Hassan

CONTENTS

4.1 Introduction 66
4.2 Internet of Things (IoT) 67
4.3 IoT Infrastructure 68
    4.3.1 Components 68
        4.3.1.1 Identification Block 68
        4.3.1.2 Sensing Block 68
        4.3.1.3 Communication Block 68
        4.3.1.4 Computation Block 69
        4.3.1.5 Service Block and Semantics Block 69
    4.3.2 Protocols 69
    4.3.3 Applications 73
        4.3.3.1 Home Automation 74
        4.3.3.2 Smart Agriculture 74
        4.3.3.3 eHealth 74
        4.3.3.4 Logistics 75
4.4 Deep Learning in Gaming and Animation 75
    4.4.1 MotionScan Technology 77
    4.4.2 Framework (Architectural Model) 77
    4.4.3 Appearance Model 78
4.5 IoT and 5G Technology 78
4.6 Artificial Intelligence 79
    4.6.1 Supervised Learning 80
        4.6.1.1 Regression 81
        4.6.1.2 Classification 81

DOI: 10.1201/9781003231530-4

4.7 Discussion on Machine Learning and Data Analytics in IoT Networks........ 83
4.8 Trends and Challenges.. 87
4.9 Conclusion 88
References... 88

4.1 INTRODUCTION

Thanks to Internet technology which has brought various new concepts and opportunities to life. Today the Internet of Things (IoT) concept has become a fast-growing industry in developed and developing countries. Due to Internet availability, we can access instant real-world devices and digital information anywhere at any time. With the Internet's help, most of our daily usage things are connected us while we are away from home; for example, watches, home TVs, kids monitoring, house monitoring, air conditioners, car and many more. Therefore, IoT industry's rapid growth needs reliable IoT applications, protocols, and platforms to support future industries such as smart cities, smart homes, smart appliances, gaming, e-health, logistics, and intelligent forming requirements.

IoT can be recognized as a network of neighboring things that connect via Internet to share collected information without requiring human-to-human or human-to-computer interaction. It is a network combination of many tiny sensor devices which sense and collect various information depending on their characteristics and transmit to the respective user via a wireless medium. The environmental and physical parameters are sensed and monitored to take pre-defined actions. Users can access live data, instantly notified to take appropriate measures.

IoT networks offer several benefits to various industries. According to an IDC forecast, there will be 41.6 billion IoT devices connected over the Internet by 2025, which will generate approximately 79.4 zettabytes (ZB) amount of data [1].

IoT systems include numerous business applications to offer many benefits to humankind. The new Industrial IoT and the fourth digital revolution (Industry 4.0) provide designers and implementers' versatility and increase their decision-making abilities using IoT and machine learning (ML) developments. Besides ML, cloud computing services provide more benefit to companies and individual in term of usability and productivity.

Artificial intelligence (AI) and ML techniques facilitate the communication between systems, allowing them to make their own autonomous choices [2]. A simple IoT Network is used to offer self-optimized networks service. The individually designed network is expected to be configured for massive data transfer and reception between a various autonomous device with time and channel free freedom. The connected devices will determine and calculate the shortest flow path for successful transmission. AI make these devices more efficient and communicate with each other effectively.

In the field of gaming, opponents of human players often have advanced AI involving genetic algorithms (GA). Strategies used in the past are being programmed using AI to ensure that AI can learn and develop from past experiences. Learning techniques allow AI to repeat past mistakes, enhance the game. This allows for a more realistic experience for human players as they need to change their strategy over time. It also helps to avoid situations where the human player finds a sequence of moves that ultimately leads to success, meaning that the game no longer becomes a challenge. GA an instance is needed to illustrate the challenges in the solution situation and the optimal process of determining the quality of the example. The fitness function first recognizes the variability of a unit and determines its properties. In addition, these special functions are tailored to the problem domain. The fitness function can only be a system timing function in most cases, especially code optimization. As genetic representation and fitness functions are determined, GA create an initial candidate sample that will then apply multiple repeat operators with options, crossovers, and options to increase the value of the candidate's fitness.

This chapter has discussed the deep learning (DL) involvement in IoT networks, components, application, protocols, gaming and expectation from 5G network. We have discussed the various ML; DA algorithms and concepts enhance the IoT network productivity and efficiency. In the last part, we have discussed the future trend and challenges.

4.2 INTERNET OF THINGS (IoT)

In the last two eras, IoT-based networks have become famous and utilized in many industries such as agriculture, medical, manufacture, and so on due to their usability and performance. Wireless Sensor Network (WSN) is one example of IoT base network that can be utilized in many areas. Throughout the years, WSNs have been implemented for smart agriculture, emphasizing environmental tracking, precision cultivation, system, process management automation and traceability. WSN's offers self-manage, self-configure, self-diagnosis, and self-heal rendered as intelligent agriculture monitoring network. The WSN is a device made up of transceivers, cameras, microcontrollers, and radio frequency (RF) sources. However, when IoT became a significant force in smart agriculture, it has shifted the model from using the WSN for smart agriculture to IoT. The IoT integrates other established innovations, including WSN, RF recognition, cloud storage, middleware platforms, and end-user software [3]. The goal of IoT in agriculture and other industries is to empower farmers with decision-making tools and automation technology that seamlessly combine resources, information, and services to increase production, efficiency, and revenue. Latest studies have centered on obstacles and restrictions faced by IoT and WSN industries to manage and handle large amounts of data for a long time that required new innovative models, analysis techniques, data protection and safety, and proper data management approaches to take current obstacles. The usage of WSNs has become a key component in several industries [3].

Multi-player online skill games are popularly played for money and offer a perfect form of fun and leisure. To ensure ethically responsible gaming, service providers that have interactive environments for playing social games for real money must contribute to detecting and avoiding potentially dangerous addictive behaviors. To put it another way, when playing cash, use care and decision [4].

Recent IoT solutions offer market share and provide competitive advantages and usability for consumers to use it and promote preference. It offers a range of resources and technologies, such as data collection and processing, system management, convergence, surveillance, user visibility into processes, and capacity to recognize and handle these apps. There are various IoT types, such as on-site applications, which run on the same premises and networks as off-site systems that usually utilize cloud storage. Companies also pick based on these templates.

4.3 IoT INFRASTRUCTURE

4.3.1 COMPONENTS

Usually, IoT associated networks are a combination of the large number of devices connected worldwide. IoT technology connects smart devices, gateways, data networks via cloud computing and applications. These intelligent devices are mostly at various distance from each other under multiple scenarios and controlled by the centralized management system to process and save the data or information. Entire IoT infrastructure is made of various elements, blocks, components, and protocols. IoT components consist of a sensing unit, a communication unit, computation, and Internet (connectivity) unit and appropriate protocols and services. In addition to featured features and application capabilities, IoT communication protocols, computational processing speed, and cloud services define IoT platforms, strengths, and limitations [5]. The growing demand and involvement of IoT in recent industries signify the interoperability improvement needs between various applications and services as per user requirements. IoT infrastructure model consists of six blocks such as [5]:

4.3.1.1 Identification Block

Each IoT object must have a unique ID and connected to the IoT network infrastructure properly.

4.3.1.2 Sensing Block

Includes sensors to sense and observe the physical environment parameters. IoT network's main objective is to keep and access the physical environmental parameters in any industry mainly completed by sensor nodes deployed in vast or small areas. These sensor nodes sense physical environmental values such as temperature, humidity, air pressure, etc., and convert them into electrical signals and transmit. The sensing system collects the sensed data and forwards to a connected network, such as the data management system. Other algorithms are then applied for data validation and visualization. Mostly information is transmitted via Internet and saved via cloud computing infrastructure. Sensing unit also contains actuators which are connected by wires or wireless medium as part of network objects. Actuators are mechanical hardware devices such as switches, gateway, etc. that used in IoT platforms. These devices get the user's instruction or the sensors and perform appropriate actions such as open/close windows, doors, curtain, light on/off, etc. Actuator devices convert electrical signals into physical measures.

4.3.1.3 Communication Block

To transmit the data over a wireless or wired medium. The communication unit is another aspect of IoT network. All connected sensor nodes should communicate with each other especially with the upper system that handles the collected data. A gateway or bridge is used in a condition when connected devices cannot adequately communicate with other systems via a specific protocol. Therefore, a gateway is used to communicate among various network via communication protocols. The IoT devices used several communication technologies such as WiFi, ZigBee, Near Field Communication (NFC), Bluetooth Low-Energy (BLE), Long Term Evolution (LTE), LoRa, SigFox, NarrowBand (NB)-IoT, etc., to connect with the Internet. Hence, in IoT networks identification methods are considered better than authentication in terms of performance gains. For different recognition technologies, each entity is unique through its recognition [6]. There are several communication protocols used in IoT networks such as Constrained Application Protocol (CoAP) and Message Queue Telemetry Transport (MQTT) to connect IoT objects with the data management system.

4.3.1.4 Computation Block

Responsible for computing and processing data. In the IoT network, mostly data is stored on the cloud network to access it from anywhere and anytime. There are various protocols, technologies used for data management services. Sensing devices send the data to the respective data server mostly stored on the cloud and perform computational tasks.

4.3.1.5 Service Block and Semantics Block

Offers Internet connectivity and data analytics and ML techniques to get relevant results from the collected data. These techniques help the user to visualize, manage and secure the appropriate data. As a service, networking is offered by the free use of apps. Data obtained by the sensors and devices can be used for analytical tools in application creation.

4.3.2 Protocols

IoT protocol can be divided into two basic types such as IoT Network Protocol related to managing the network traffic and IoT Data Protocols related to managing data availability. In the IoT network, the connected devices are not entirely machine-to-machine M2M systems because M2M communication devices directly communicate. In M2M communication, devices such as sensor, actuators, and embedded systems capture or sense the data and share with other connected devices. For example, they controlled electrical applications like bulbs, air conditioner, fridge and fan RF or Bluetooth technology using smartphones or remotes. Therefore, electrical appliance and smartphones considered as two different machines which are interacting with each other. However, in IoT networks, physical devices are embedded with sensors, software, and electronics to communicate using a cloud base or Internet-related network. IoT networks are about sensor automation and Internet platform [7]. Figure 4.1 shows the concept difference of M2M and IoT.

In IoT network, most of the system parts need to be configured, maintained, and monitored to offer expected services and data management [7].

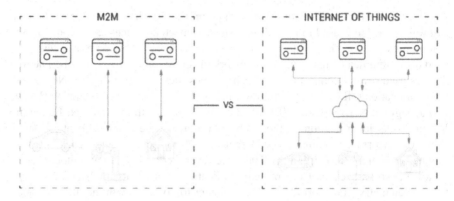

FIGURE 4.1   Difference of M2M and IoT [7].

CoAP is a new communication protocol mainly designed for IoT networks, low power devices. It allows connected devices to communicate among themselves and with the Internet using similar protocols. Its lightweight generator traffic and intended to use for resource-constrained Internet devices such as sensor nodes. It is a service layer protocol that offers one to one communication like Hypertext Transfer Protocol (HTTP) and does not support TCP/IP. It uses User Datagram Protocol (UDP) over IP to offer efficiency as compared to HTTP. It uses fewer resources than HTTP and provides more observation, execution, discovery, reading, and writing. CoAP is the best choice for web services based [8].

MQTT is another communication protocol that is used in IoT networks. It was developed in 1999 by Arlen Nipper (Arcom) and Andy Stanford-Clark (IBM) to collect data from various electrical devices. It is mostly used for monitoring from a remote area in IoT networks [8]. It is implemented over TCP/IP as a lightweight communication protocol and work on a hub-and-spoke architecture concept. The correspondence between devices uses a message brokers' server that does not make an M2M communication platform. It utilized three elements such as subscriber, publisher, and a broker. MQTT support Secure Sockets Layer (SSL) and Transport Layer Security (TLS) for security services. In WAN IoT base networks, MQTT is considered better to use due to its broker concept. The broker is a center point of contact between sensor devices. MQTT protocol is a favorite choice for all IoT based devices because it provides ample routing information functions to cheap, memory-intensive, and small devices on low and poor bandwidth-based networks. It is useful for poor bandwidth networks, especially in numerous remote locations. Therefore, Amazon and Microsoft Azure are using the MQTT protocol for their services.

Bluetooth is one of the most used short-distance wireless technologies used in IoT networks. User can get Bluetooth applications that offer wearable technology to connect smart devices quickly. One of the newly developed Bluetooth protocol for IoT networks is known as Bluetooth Low-Energy (BLE) protocol as shown in Figure 4.2. It offers the same services as Bluetooth with lower power consumption. However, BLE is not designed to transfer large files and is mainly preferable for small file size [9].

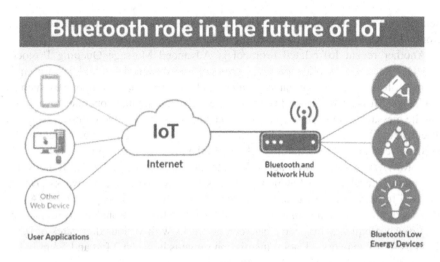

FIGURE 4.2   Bluetooth Communication.

WiFi is another famous and favored IoT network-related protocol and accepted by many industries because it offers fast data transfer speeds and many data. The large WiFi 802.11 standard allows user to transmit hundreds of megabits in a second only. However, WiFi technology consumes a considerable amount of battery that is one of its drawbacks. It operates on 2.4 GHz and 5 GHz frequencies band [9, 10].

ZigBee is another protocol which is mainly designed for IoT related industries as compared to the consumers. It operates mostly on the 2.4 GHz frequency band with a smaller data transmission rate [9, 10].

The Data Distribution Service (DDS) is another standard protocol choice for the high-efficiency, expandable and efficient machine-to-machine communication. It is developed by Objective Management Group. Users can transfer data on both low-scale devices and cloud services using DDS. It used two important layers such as Data-Centric Publish-Subscribe (DCPS) and Data Local Reconstruction Layer (DLRL). The DCPS used to deliver information to the subscribers, and DLRL offer an interface to DCPS [9].

NFC is another IoT related technology that is mostly used in the latest mobile phones. It allows users to connect with electronic devices to use digital contents to perform contactless payment transactions. It mainly emphasis on contactless communication between electronic devices. It has a minimal distance range of 4 cm between both electronic devices [9].

Many IoT applications are available to call for service over a longer distance. The use of cellular networking technologies such as 4G/5G is possible in such IoT applications. Cellular is an IoT Communication Protocol that can send or transmit a large quantity of data over the longer distance. However, users must understand the cost of the cellular network, which might be quite expensive and consume more power. Therefore, SparqEE has introduced a cellular kit with a name CELLv1.0 which can be used in Arduino and Raspberry Pi platforms to get the cellular technology benefits in IoT related networks. CELLv1.0 used a 2G+3G chipset to communicate worldwide with longer distance and lower battery consumption [11].

Another recent IoT-related protocol is Advanced Message Queuing Protocol (AMQP) known as application layer protocol and designed for middleware environment. It is a message-oriented protocol and has three main components such as Exchange, Message Queue and Binding. The Exchange segment operates by arranging the message in the queues. The Message Queue is responsible for processing the directive until the client's app safely creates the message. The linking element of the exchange component indicates the relation to the message queue portion [9].

LoRaWAN is a wide area network protocol which is also used in IoT network. It is mainly developed for low power devices to serve many node networks primarily used in heavy networks such as smart cities or similar concepts. LoRaWAN is also recognized in many industries for protecting bi-directional communication. LoRaWAN frequency may vary between networks with various data rates of 0.3 – 50 kbps in IoT networks. Data transmission range is between 2 km and 5 km in the urban areas approximately 15 km in the suburban areas [9].

The Radio Frequency Identification (RFID) is another wireless technology used in low power IoT short-range networks. RFID used the Active Reader Active Tag system that does not require any power. This technology used an electromagnetic field to identify the smart device or objects and the Radiofrequency communication range is around 10 cm to 200 mm [9].

Z-Wave IoT networks Protocol communicate on low-energy radiofrequency and mainly used in home automation systems. This low latency technology also has more wireless security features and is used for low power RF devices such as sensors, lamp controllers, etc. Z-Wave used 900 MHz frequency and have a 30–100 m range with 40–100 kbit/s data rates [9].

On top of all, SigFox is recognized as one of the best solutions with cellular and WiFi characteristics. It is designed for M2M applications to transmit low-level data. It can handle 10–1000 bits per second transfer speed using Ultra Narrow Band (UNB) and consume only 50 microwatts of the power. It also runs on 900 MHz frequency and has cloud access. SigFox ranges are between 30–50 km in rural areas and 3–10 km in the urban areas.

Thread is another new IoT security protocol created by Thread Group and getting famous in-home automation applications. It is IPv6 network protocol based on the 6LowPAN. It was mainly designed to complement indoor Wi-Fi networks with the benefit of free protocol. It supports mess topology structure and uses IEEE802.15.4. It runs on 2.4 GHz (ISM) frequency band ad cover 10–20 m distance for data transmission. It can handle approximately 250 nodes by having encryption and authentication features.

EnOcean takes an innovative spin under the IoT Protocols. It is ideal for designing networks that need quick response in various circumstances such as temperature changes, humidity, lighting, and others. It runs on multiple frequencies such as 315 MHz, 868 MHz, and 902 MHz and covers 300 m communication range for outdoor and 30 m range for indoors networks. This protocol is currently being used in various industries such as transportation, home and industrial automation, logistics, and others [9]. In Figure 4.3, we can observe the operating layer model of IoT protocols and their services [12].

Application Layer	Operating Systems	Contiki	Tiny OS	Riot OS	Lite OS	Android
	Services	Smart City { Building, Transport, Traffic }	Environment { Natural Resources, Disaster }	Law	Health Care	Industrial / Power Grid
	Protocols	**MQTT**	**CoAP**	**XMPP**	**AMQP**	**DDS**
Network Layer	Routing Protocol	Routing Protocol for Low Power and Lossy Networks (RPL)				
	Network Protocol	6LowPAN		IPV6		
	Link Related Technology	IEEE 802.15.4				
Objects Layer (Perception)	Sensors and Actuators	Arduino	Raspberry Pi	ESP8266	Beaglebone Black	Intel Edison	Telos B
	Physical Layer Protocols	Zigbee	EPCglobal	IEEE 802.15.4	Z-Wave	BLE
	Device Communication Technologies	RFID	GSM	Infrared	UMTS	LTE-A	5G

FIGURE 4.3 IoT operating layer model.

4.3.3 APPLICATIONS

IoT field is still emerging technology, but it helps many industries play important roles [13]. While IoT is an evolving area, it has helped to enhance numerous applications that have changed our lives in many ways. The IoT-I project 2010 survey described 65 IoT scenarios covering 12 areas: travel, smart home, smart city, lifestyle, gaming, agriculture, supply chains, emergency services, public health care, user engagement, culture and tourism, climate, and environment [14]. The IoT analytical web portal results show the growing number of IoT projects in various worldwide regions [15]. In Figure 4.4, we can observe the ever-increasing number of IoT involved in multiple industries. Smart City and Industries are on top with the heavy usage of IoT-related networks.

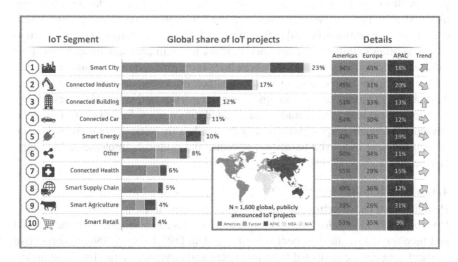

FIGURE 4.4 Top 10 IoT involved industries.

4.3.3.1   Home Automation

Using IoT network in the home environment helps manage and control user life and enhance daily life product productivity. Individual users and companies can get any data that could be used for many useful purposes such as understanding the user health, daily activities, electricity usage, kids monitoring, monitoring common house problems, etc. Furthermore, the bedrooms' heating can be adjusted to the needs and conditions of the environment using IoT networks. Rooms lighting and air-conditioner usage can be controlled and monitored on a timely basis. IoT devices will automatically off/on and maintain electrical appliances such as fridges and air-conditioners to save electric power. The washing machine consisting of master RFID readers and slave readers will recognize dirty clothes and wash them automatically using RFID tags to collect resentful information on color, contents, and a suitable washing program. In kitchens for the cooking equipment's, to automate similar cooking technologies can be used. IoT network also can boost home security to a large extent. High-level security devices such as smoke alarm, camera, and an infrared detector, can be used with the latest security dynamics. The user can view the home anytime from anywhere using an Internet connection [13].

4.3.3.2   Smart Agriculture

Today, the agriculture industry is also expanding and taking advantage of new industry standards and platforms with the Internet and technology growth. The development of IoT networks has reformed the entire agriculture industry into a new era. In a traditional agricultural concept, crops are planted into a large paddy field area, and farmers used to inspect regularly crops parameters such as growth, diseases attacks, water level, humidity, temperature and so on, by visiting the paddy field themselves which was a solemn and hectic task especially in a bad weather condition [13]. However, now with IoT networks and WSN, these monitoring tasks have become easy for farmers. They do not need to regularly visit the paddy field and periodically monitor the data from home using IoT-based networks. Furthermore, using AI and Data Analytical knowledge, the deployed networks can predict future data trend base on the collected data figures [16]. The weather, humidity, wind, pressure, and other details can be obtained in real-time with accuracy using WSN. This information could use to improve agriculture crop production and quality control. For example, by understanding future weather information, farmers can choose ways and precautions to enhance and control the fruits and vegetables. Besides, by monitoring soil moisture, humidity, and related information, farmers can control the amount of sugar in grapes plants and grapevine health. Various companies produce several kinds of industrial hardware, systems, and protocols implemented for agriculture monitoring [17, 18].

4.3.3.3   eHealth

Health industry also getting optimal benefits from the usability of the IoT network. Due to the ubiquitous IoT network capacities, all devices connected can be tracked and monitored to collect respective and live data [19]. Using WSNs, patients' live medical data can be collected from anywhere and anytime, saving lives and understanding the variable parameters. Several AI-based smart applications such as live heath monitoring or fall detection, diet monitoring, body mass index (BMI) monitoring, blood pressure and heartbeat monitoring helps older people and disabled people to live independently. With the help of these smart devices and applications, doctors can continuously and effectively monitor patients' health over the longer distance. The growing rate of ageing has created many healthcare problems in today era. For instance, some countries have old-houses and rehabilitation centers that manage old age people or sick people and offer health services. IoT networks help in these areas to continuously control and monitor patients' health parameters [13].

Google Health application was released in 2008 as a personal health monitor application. The application allows users to share their personal health information with health service providers voluntarily. The Google Health application gets input from users or monitors the user's health and generates a complete report on its health record. Later, the application was upgraded, and the user's records are synchronized on the cloud for further analysis. In the current era, various patient monitoring and hospital-orientated systems are designed, developed, and significant changes have been made to incorporate multidisciplinary information fields [20].

4.3.3.4 Logistics

Like other fields, transport and logistics industries are also taking advantages of IoT systems. IoT helps the transportation industry improve transport efficiency and precision across the entire supply chain, real-time monitoring and object movements tracking from source to destination using attached RFID tags. In addition, IoT provides promising solutions for transforming transport and can predict vehicles moving in parking or on the road. For example, BMW, Honda, and other vehicle manufacture companies used several sensors and tags to monitor the environment to provide drivers with driving direction with an intelligent computer system. Moreover, other transportation and logistics operations such as routes control, warning emission, track monitoring, etc., can also be enhanced by IoT [13]. Overall, IoT applications can be grouped into 54 primary application containing 12 main domains due to their usability and involvement in many industries [15].

4.4   DEEP LEARNING IN GAMING AND ANIMATION

Researchers from the University of Edinburgh and Adobe Research have created an AI that video game characters can use to communicate more naturally with their surroundings. This method employs a "Neural State Machine" (NSM) which is a deep neural network that predicts a character's movement in each scene. Character animation was very simple in the days of 8- and 16-bit video games, with most games featuring a stable world and dialogue. As a result, the avatar action does not necessitate a vast number of separate animations. The challenge of making animations became more difficult with the introduction of 3D games. Now gaming technology has grown to include a wide-open world and the potential to communicate with it, animating a character requires hundreds or thousands of different movement abilities as shown in Figure 4.5. Using motion capture (mo-cap) to digitize the actor's gestures into character-appropriate animation is one way to lighten and speed up the saturation of the animation process. As a result, the game's action seems to be more

FIGURE 4.5 IoT application and industries.

believable. However, understanding the single way the player communicates with the world is almost impossible.

Furthermore, the switch between animations can look clunky and canned. Changes between moves are usually done by reusable algorithms that work in the same way every time. Consider how a character could sit in a chair or place a box. This is made more difficult as the objects are in varying sizes. Picking up things in various shapes and sizes or resting your arms on seats of various sizes may be uncomfortable. A variety of moves should be considered and animated when moving an object, including beginning to walk, slowing down, turning appropriately when positioning the foot, and engaging with the object. At the same time, our.ng produces a wide range of high-quality moves and actions from a single network. NSM has been taught how to transition from one movement to the next in a normal manner. Based on the previous poses and scenario geometry, the network advances the next character.

Mo-cap is the process of recording people's real-life movements with a camera aimed at capturing those precise movements in a scene created by a computer camera. As someone who is fascinated using this technology in game development to create animations, it was great to see the major improvement achieved with DL. I was delighted to see the great improvements that have been made to this technology with the help of DL [21].

4.4.1 MotionScan Technology

That was back in 2011 when L.A. Noir really brought a great life-like face animation that looks ahead of every other game. Now, almost a decade later, we still have not seen many other games close to the level when it comes to displaying facial expressions [22].

L.A. in 2011 to create life-like face animations. MotionScan technology used by Rockstar Studios in Noir. This is because the face scanning technology used in the development of this game, called MotionScan, is very expensive and the file size of the captured animation is very large, which is why most publishers use this technology for their games. However, this may soon change due to recent advances in mo-cap driven by in-depth training.

In the following research work, the authors introduce a DL Framework for creating animations from the source image of a face, following the movements of another face in a moving video like MotionScan technology. They propose a self-monitoring training method that can use labelled video data without a specific category to study the significant dynamics that define movement. Then show how those motion dynamics can be combined with static imagery to create motion videos [23].

4.4.2 Framework (Architectural Model)

DL Framework architect template in Figure 4.6 shows a motion module and a visual module [23]. Drive is the input of the video motion module and the source image is our target object which is the input of the visual module.

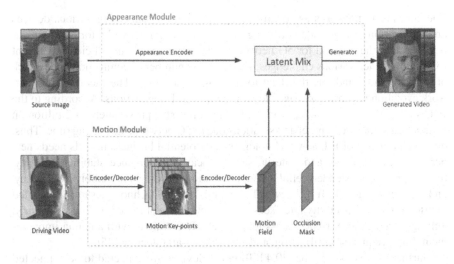

FIGURE 4.6   First order model framework.

Motion module has an encoder that must study the incredible presentation which contains important key points that are very important in relation to the motion of the object, which is the face in this view. The motion of these key points in different frames of the driving video creates an area of motion, driven by the function that we want to study our model. The author uses the Taylor expansion to predict this process from the first order that builds this plane of motion. According to the authors, this is the first time a first-order approach has been used to model movement. In addition, a solid motion field is created by combining the studied Eiffen transformations of these keys. A solid motion plane predicts the speed of each pixel of distance, not just focusing on the main points of the sparse motion plane. In addition, the Motion Module also generates an acceleration map, highlighting the frame pixels that need to be painted [24].

4.4.3 Appearance Model

Visual Module uses an encoder to encode the source image, which is combined with a motion field and acceleration map to animate the source image. Generator models are used for this purpose. During the self-examined learning process, a style frame from the driving video is used as the source image and the studied motion plane is used to scent the source image. Since the actual video frame serves as the truth for the movement of the results, this is self-monitoring training. During the testing estimate phase, this source image can be replaced with another image of the same object category, and it does not need to come from the driving video [24].

There are several DL applications in the current market such as Self Driving Cars, Entertainment, Visual Recognition, Virtual Assistants, and Natural Language Processing.

4.5 IoT AND 5G TECHNOLOGY

The current 4G networks are continuously evolving by connecting various devices and application. IoT was also utilizing the benefits of 4G networks for communication. It raises the demand for 5G networks with better speed and efficiency. Current IoT solutions face various challenges, such as large number of connection nodes, lack of security and standards that lead to the Internet's future. The incoming 5G network evolution was bringing significant growth in IoT applications. According to the IDC study, 70% of companies worldwide would invest approximately $1.2 billion on connectivity-management related solutions due to 5G networks in coming time. Thus, due to emergence of IoT new technologies and potential business models needs new performance standards and criteria, such as heavy convergence stability, security, throughput, more extended cellular communications coverage, incredibly low latency, and more efficiency. To fulfill new IoT standards, the 5G technologies are anticipated to offer unique connectivity interfaces. The development of incoming 5G is still early, aiming to run on new radio access technology (RAT) along with antenna improvement, high frequencies utilization, and networks re-architecting [25].

Gartner expresses [25] that 20.4 billion IoT devices are expected to be connected online by the end of 2020. The 5G evolution will bring more devices online to meet

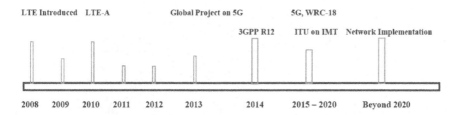

FIGURE 4.7 Wireless network growth.

the market demand of IoT networks in the coming time, to stimulate new social development and economics needs. The emerging conditions of potential IoT networks and the advancement of 5G wireless technologies are two significant developments that propel the 5G IoT [25]. At present, the IoT networks use 3G and 4G networks extensively but not entirely optimized by IoT applications. The 4G generation refers to LTE with significant capabilities to offer various Internet base services for IoT networks. 4G network are more reliable, fast, and provide consistent services to users than other technologies such as BLE, WiMaxB, ZigBee, SigFox, LoRa, and others [20]. However, with the proliferation of IoT networks and applications, 5G networks are expected to offer fast and sustainable Internet services. Figure 4.7 shows the mobile network evolution from 3G to coming 5G enables IoT generation [25].

The new 5G networks are expected to operate exclusively on 4G LTE core network to offer, data and Internet services with the speed of 10Gbps along connecting thousands of devices. A lot of academic and industrial research are going on to understand various aspects of IoT and 5G networks. The main objective is to enhance the productivity of the IoT network using 5G technology. In a collaboration project involving CISCO, Intel, and Verizon, 5G has unveiled a novel series of "neuroscience-based algorithms" that adaptive video quality to the human eye's demand, indicating that the wireless networks are integrated into human intelligence. The 5G generation will contribute to IoT success by connecting thousands of intelligent devices and interacting without human participation. The 5G-IoT networks are expected to offer real-time, on-demand, re-configurable services that required the 5G-IoT architecture to provide smart operations on each phase. The 5G-IoT networks are expected to offer [25]:

- Offer a logically independent network as per application requirements.
- Provide a large connection of various standards and implement the on-demand deployment of RAN by using cloud base radio access network.
- Simplify core network architecture to implement the on-demand configuration of network functions.

4.6 ARTIFICIAL INTELLIGENCE

By considering industries and user expectation from the IoT, scientists and data engineer brought AI concept to IoT [26]. AI is the science of teaching knowledge into the machine to execute tasks that the human mind traditionally demanded and need time

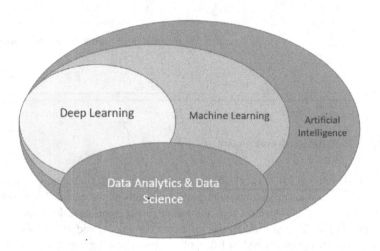

FIGURE 4.8   Overview of AI.

to complete. Due to heavy demand for AI applications and equipment, implementations, configurations, operational speed, and functionality of AI-based systems are developing rapidly. A variety of disciplines have been integrated to improve AI's interdisciplinary aspect, such as economics, computational sciences, engineering, statistics, genetics, physics, sociology, psychology, and several more. Intelligence is obtained from all the data produced in these areas. To understand the values behind this data, proper interpretation is necessary.

AI strongly depends on data science, ML, and data analytic field. In simply, data science is the study of designing techniques and methods to interpret and extract knowledge from vast data quantities. Discipline is also a blend of several other fields of study. Software developed concepts come predominantly from computer science, primarily concerned with efficient algorithmic performance and data management scalability. AI concepts come from far more different fields for research. AI techniques used as a methodology for optimally utilizing data can be accessed by the individuals and should be able to update and modify to describe in a meaningful manner [5].

Architecture and technology for digital devices built with Internet connectivity in keeping with the IoT definition will be highly scalable. The network must be supplied, keeping in mind the complexity of technologies and the constant need for seamless connectivity. Just as in the IoT model interpretation, it is not obvious how to construct its architecture. Many general IoT network solutions exist, but not all of them are robust enough [5].

4.6.1   SUPERVISED LEARNING

Supervised learning is one of ML most effective method of data analysis. The user provides the set of inputs and outputs to find the relation between them through the system training. Later, the user can get a function from an input x with the best estimation of output y such as ($f: x \rightarrow y$). The significant task of supervised learning algorithms is to construct a model that describes relationship and dependency connections between inputs and forecast objective outputs. It is used in many applications to solve various problems such as in WSN. It helps to solve routing, localization, fault detection, data aggregation, congestion and energy harvesting related issues. It can be different categories into two sub-categories, such as Classification and Regression [26].

4.6.1.1 Regression

This method predicts some value (Y) based on a given set of parameters (X) along with continuous or quantitative variables. It is a simple ML method used to predict accurate results with fewer errors.

Linear Regression: The purpose of linear regression is to learn a function f that is mapping with Y value. It can be represented with the following mathematical model. In the equation, Y refers to the dependent variable (output), x represents independent variable (input), f refers to a function that makes the relation between x and Y, and ε deal with an expected random error.

$$Y = f(x) + \varepsilon$$

Support Vector Regression (SVR): The Support Vector Machine (SVM) method is used to solve regression problems along a process known as SVR.

4.6.1.2 Classification

Classification can be further divided into various fields.

- **Decision Trees (DT):** DTs comes under supervised ML technique of classification using if-then rules, and it is used to improve the data readability. A DL consist of two nodes known as leaf and decision nodes. The DT is used to predict a class or outcome by creating a training model based on decision rules inferred from training data. These techniques are more transparent, reduce ambiguity in decision-making and offer a comprehensive analysis. DTs are used to solve connectivity, anomaly detection, data aggregation, mobile sink path selection related problems in WSNs. An example of DT is shown in Figure 4.9.

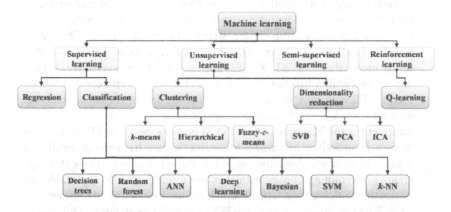

FIGURE 4.9 Machine learning algorithm.

FIGURE 4.10   Decision tree example.

- **Random Forest (RF):** RF techniques are supervised ML methods that used trees collection, and each tree represents a classification or value. This algorithm works in two steps, the creation of RF classifier and prediction of the results. These algorithms mainly used effectively in larger datasets and heterogeneous datasets. These algorithms primarily used to solve coverage and MAC protocol-related problems in WSNs.
- **Artificial Neural Networks (ANN):** ANN is another supervised ML technique using human neuron model to classify the data. It contains many neurons to process information and produce accurate results. It used three layers that relate to nodes, and each node is associated with an active function. Each ANN connected with three layers such as input layer, hidden layer, and output layer. ANN easily can classify complex and non-liner data sets without any input instructions. ANN techniques are used to enhance the efficiency of WSN is several areas such as localization, node failure deduction, congestion, routing, and data aggregation.
- **Deep Learning (DL):** DL is another ML technique used for classification and comes under ANN. DL use multi-layers' data representation and composed with a simple non-linear module. It can work with or without labels to extract high-level objectives from the data. DL methodology is used in various domain such as Business Intelligence, Social Network Analysis, Biotechnology, Medical and many more. It also being used in WSNs to solve routing, data quality estimation, energy distribution, and fault detection related problems.
- **Bayesian:** Bayesian is another supervised ML technique that used a statistical learning method to find the dataset's relationships by learning the conditional independent using various statistical methods such as Chi-square test. It takes the set of inputs $X1, X2, X3, X4, \ldots, Xn$ and returns a label θ, the probability $P(\theta \mid X1, X2, X3, X4, \ldots, Xn)$ to be maximize. It uses various probability functions for different class nodes variables. It has been used in WSNs to solve event detection, routing, data aggregation, tracking, path selection and synchronization aspects.
- **Support Vector Machine (SVM):** SVM is also supervised ML techniques that search an optimal hyperplane to classify the data. It is a non-probabilistic, binary classifier which mainly use to find the dividing hyperplane that separates both training classes with maximum margin. SVM is suitable for interacting with learning tasks in which the number of training instances is large. SVM techniques are used in WSNs to solve localization, fault detection, congestion, routing, and localization related problems.

TABLE 4.1

Overview of ML Algorithm used in IoT Networks

Overview of ML Algorithm used in IoT Networks

ML Algorithm	IoT Network Use Case	Data Set to Optimize
Classification	Smart Traffic	Traffic Prediction
Clustering	Smart Traffic, Smart Health	Traffic Prediction
Anomaly Detection	Smart Traffic, Smart Environment	Traffic Prediction
Support Vector Regression	Smart Weather Prediction	Forecasting
Linear Regression and Regression Trees	Economics, Market Analysis, Smart Citizen	Real time Prediction
SVM	Various Data	Real time Prediction
k-NN	Smart Citizen	Passengers Travel Pattern
Naïve Bayes	Smart Citizen, Agriculture	Food Safety, Passengers Travel Pattern

- **k-Nearest Neighbor (k-NN):** It is one of the straightforward laziest instance-based learning techniques in regression and classification. In this algorithm, the K nearest training set is considered input from the feature space and classifies based on the distance between specified training samples and sample tests. It utilized different distance functions such as Canberra distance, Euclidean distance, Manhattan distance, Hamming distance, and many more. This method's complexity depends on the size and optimal output of the input dataset for the same data scale. This method defines function space for potential missed values and therefore eliminates dimensionality. It mainly used to optimize fault detection and data aggregation problem in WSNs.

Table 4.1 shows the overview of ML algorithm used in IoT Network [27, 28].

4.7 DISCUSSION ON MACHINE LEARNING AND DATA ANALYTICS IN IoT NETWORKS

ML and Data Analytics are two most prominent techniques that have been used in all industries to optimize the outcome and future predictions. Both methods are vastly used in various sectors, especially have become common in IoT networks. In co-operative ML and IoT, better connectivity and computational efficiency, controllability and decision-taking can be achieved. IoT has enormous potential to improve the quality of human life and the potential industrial application productivity, with the help of advanced monitoring from thousands to billions of ubiquitous sensor devices and improved communication capabilities. Through converging ML, AI, and data analytics, IoT ability has been dramatically increased. Advanced technology in machine intelligence has enabled a large volume of IoT sensory data to be better understood and take critical operational decisions on a range of real-world problems. To resolve world complex problems and satisfy the computation and communication needs, IoT and

ML must balance each other and effectively fulfill them. The popularity and demand for data analytics also have increased in recent years, along with the ML algorithm.

ML integration in the IoT field has opened new productivity, efficiency, economical, and accuracy IoT solutions. ML usability in IoT applications improves communication and computational performance, better controllability, and enhances decision-making skills. IoT networks consist of thousands to billion ubiquitous sensing devices to offer reliable and consistent communication to improve and secure society lifestyle and industry workflow. Recently, IoT application has significantly improved with the convergence of ML and AI techniques. Latest ML and AI techniques allow user easily to observe the collected data and make critical operational decisions rapidly. Therefore, in many industries, ML and AI techniques are being used to make the rapid and successful decision based on collected data. Today, Data Analytics has got significant attention in IoT network due to the following reasons [29]:

- **Massive Volume of Data Generated from IoT devices:** Large number of devices are connected within a one IoT network. They are producing high volume data that make hard for the user to maintain and understand. Therefore, it is essential to use intelligent data analytic techniques to extract relevant data rapidly.
- **Variability in Huge Volume Data Collected from Heterogeneous Devices:** In IoT network, many devices are connected and processing the information among themselves. Due to IoT network heterogeneity, data quality, processing, and storage have been considered challenging tasks to handle.
- **Data Uncertainty:** In IoT networks, devices can change their characteristics due to certain limitations such as battery drain, network failure, path loss, interference, and others. Uncertainty is considered standard in practical data analysis. Data loss is always present in IoT, which needs efficient analytics techniques to pre-process the data. It is essential to use proper analytical techniques and assessment models to enhance decision-making accuracy based on collected data.
- **Balance Scalability with the Efficiency:** Normally, IoT networks store the collected data on the cloud and perform analytics to make decisions. Moving data from smart devices to the cloud could cause a delay in transferring between different networks and speed. This could be a challenging task for time-critical application, especially in many IoT connected devices. Therefore, it is essential to manage and balance data analytics techniques accuracy and speed in many IoT networks.

Data Analytics as shown below in Figure 4.11 can be classified as following [29]:

- **Descriptive Analytics:** Normally, IoT networks collect a large amount of continuous data from a large, deployed area via smart devices. This information is stored on the cloud for user interaction. The user can generate detailed observation and opinions based on historical data collected from smart devices using appropriate ML algorithms. Descriptive analysis is defined as the method used to studies and interprets the raw data into meaningful information. Data aggregation, data mining, mathematical, logical operations, data summarization, and others are examples of descriptive analytics.

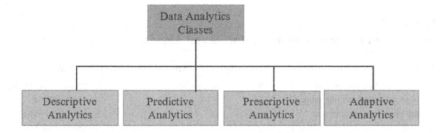

FIGURE 4.11 Data Analytics.

- **Predictive Analytics:** On the other hand, Predictive analytics utilizes historical data to model actions or patterns by utilizing predictive statistics or ML techniques to forecast the probability of possible future events or anomalies in data. In simple, it predicts future data by observing past data patterns and data correlations. It has been used in various applications to forecasts the future. Two major predictive methods, such as classification-driven models, conduct prediction studies through class membership and regression base models, are used to predict a number based on past observations and patterns. Furthermore, predictive modelling techniques include statistical regression-based models, Bayesian Analysis, DTs, and Deep Neural Network-based models.
- **Prescriptive Analytics:** This type of analysis briefs users on responding to future events based on past data analysis. It forecasts future outcomes with proper justifications. It is one of the production techniques that leverages the benefits of both descriptive and predictive analytics. These analyses are mainly used to optimize business outcomes by looking at the past and predicting future events. These techniques help the Industrial IoT setup, where business intelligence-related decisions are utilized with big data analytics and ML. Table 4.2 shows the overview of various applications using protocols, ML techniques, and analyzed data types [27, 29].
- **Adaptive Analytics:** The findings obtained from predictive analytics must be adjusted for real-time data during actual implementation. Therefore, adaptive analyses are used to adapt or optimize processes based on the latest data history and by looking at their interactions. Adaptive analysis, especially in the IoT paradigm, can be useful for processing data in real-time streams and optimizing model efficiency and minimizing errors.

To arrive at the correct decisions for intelligent data analysis, it is essential to determine the process needs to be completed out of framework exploration, locate odd data points, predict values, predict categories, or extract features. Clustering algorithms can provide the most appropriate tools for discovering the structure of unlabeled data. K-means is the most popular and often used clustering algorithm and can handle a wide range of data types with a large volume of data. Furthermore, to identify patterns and odd data points in smart data, two algorithms can be used, such as SVM and principal component analysis (PCA). Both algorithms used to offer effective results in anomalies and noisy data sets. The linear and SVR methods

TABLE 4.2

Overview of IoT Applications, Protocols and Algorithm

Application	Protocol	ML	IoT Data
Predicting energy consumption through machine learning using a Smart-Metering Architecture	MQTT, CoAP	RF	Temperature, energy consumption, humidity, wind speed – with 15 min interval
Smart City Traffic Monitoring System based on 5G Cellular Network, RFID and ML.	MQTT	Azure ML	Light, temperature, fuel consumption, magnetic, time to reach destination
Inferring occupancy from building sensors using ML	MQTT	RF	CO_2, HVAC temperature, air volume
Early detection system for gas leakage and fire in Smart home using ML	MQTT	Classification and Regression Trees	Temperature, smoke, gas, CO_2 and CO flame, humidity
Vibration condition monitoring using ML	CoAP	Neural network	Motor vibration level
Fall detection system for elderly eople using IoT and ensemble ML	MQTT, CoAP, HTTP	RF	Gyroscope data, Accelerometer data
Delay-Sensitive Health Care Data analytics at the Network Edge based on DL	CoAP	Deeping Learning	Oxygen level, plus rate, respiratory rate, sleep condition, gait tracking, washroom visit frequency
Quantifying colorimetric tests using a smartphone app based on ML classifiers	AMQP	Support Vector Machines	Blue, average, red, green values
IoT and distributed ML powered optimal state recommender solution	MQTT	Kalman filter	Heartbeat, location, acceleration
An IoT-based solution for intelligent farming	MQTT, AMQP	Rule engine	Animal posture
An IoT system to estimate personal thermal comfort	AMQP	Support Vector Machines	Heart rate, humidity, air speed, skin & room Temperature,
Integrating IoT, streaming analytics and ML to improve intelligent diabetes management system	AMQP	Azure ML	Blood sugar data
Application of ML to an Internet of Cattle	MQTT	RF, k-NN	Swaps per hour, lying time, step count
Cloud computing based smart garbage monitoring system	MQTT	Decision forest regression	Garbage level and times

are used to predict future values and to classify analyzed data. The classification and regression tree used to classify intelligent citizens' behavior is a further rapid training algorithm. Neural networks are appropriate learning models for function approximation problems to predict the categories of data [30].

4.8 TRENDS AND CHALLENGES

IoT implementations depend not only on their versatility in determining the extent of connectivity steps but also on their quick reaction to environmental change. The scheduling and predictability of IoT implementations with time restrictions may therefore play an important role mainly. There are a variety of IoT applications which must be reliable in addition to reliability. Appropriate Healthcare and avionics facilities are sources for these systems. The term "predictable" applies to the mechanisms that maintain a particular pause for the production values.

The development of IoT and wide-ranging data analytics has generated massive opportunities. AI-based IoT network has created an enormous demand in society and industries to solve several complex problems. The IoT system operating with ML algorithms have better monitoring, analyzing, and controlling data capabilities. Furthermore, it helps businesses and industries better understand upcoming challenges and make the right decisions. Although AI and IoT integration have opened several potentials, many obstacles have constrained their growth due to many reasons such as security, many ubiquitous devices, network speeds, protocols and many other.

To enhance productivity, improve decision-making, and perform future forecast analysis, the AI algorithm mainly relies on the IoT networks data. It has been observed that the application layer and transportation layer could be suspected of cyber-attacks vulnerabilities in IoT networks perception layer. Therefore, it is necessary to maintain a robust risk protection mechanism to protect the IoT network against such cyber-threats. IoT equipment requires itself attention owing to the absence of sufficient protection on certain apps. Security process in IoT networks is different as compared to traditional networks. IoT networks combine tiny size and ubiquitous devices with additional security measurement limitations due to low memory and ubiquity [27]. Therefore, the compromise between lower capability and higher security is often challenging to achieve in IoT networks. IoT network consists of a wide variety of heterogeneous nature devices that increase security risk due to mixing various vendors, types, and technological devices [31, 32].

To fulfill the Low-Power Wide-Area (LPWA) specifications, different systems such as ultra-narrowband channels and transmission bandwidth are used. As more approaches to LPWA problems are being built, innovations are needed to help higher bandwidth, long-distance coverage, a high-path error connectivity budget and longer battery life. Many NB-IoT cellular networks also allow frequency bands that run duplex dividing modes. In bands running the duplex time division modes, further research is required. These LPWA devise are required to have a robust energy-saving algorithm to achieve a longer lifetime.

Quality of Service (QoS) is expected in all IoT network levels. The opportunity to allow IoT usage in all connectivity systems through a system that wants to transmit vital data remains an active field of study [26]. Like LoRa, the use of NB-IoT networking technologies is promising robust QoS. Further research is required in the implementation of a QoS system through multiple IoT network layers.

Most robust and strong ML and DL algorithms are required to read images and extract the problem from them in the gaming and recent networks field to help the related users. Many IoT devices are connected, advanced compression and multiplexing techniques are required to share hundreds to thousands of data sizes. It is particularly needed when NB-IoT cell connectivity is used for the transmitting of images and video data. Furthermore, multiplexing allows for combining data from various sources.

In term of protocol comparison, MQTT has more reliable features as compared to CoAP. For IoT computer systems, MQTT has greater efficiency and predictability; on average, it needs 364uW higher energy consumption than CoAP to provide the same data volume. In comparison with CoAP, 4.99x is also required when using MQTT as a robust application layer protocol. Overall, the MQTT protocol is suitable for IoT systems where power and efficiency problems are not considered. CoAP has fewer reliability mechanisms and is an appropriate choice for real-time IoT systems with high power and performance constraints.

4.9   CONCLUSION

IoT consists of a wide variety of linked appliances and shares enormous data volumes. The IoT platform has been a part of our daily lives. However, IoT equipment is constrained in computational and connectivity capabilities that are bottlenecks in creating flexible, smart solutions using ML techniques. Although advancements in technology and software upgrades pave the way toward a future consisting of accelerated IoT expansion, device delivery and precise IoT data high Volume review, we also concluded that it has proved challenging to combine intelligent technologies from various fields. ML techniques play an important role in IoT networks success and assist in product enhancement. Due to IoT networks continuous growth, many improvements are required in security, data handling, processing, speed, protocols, and platform connectivity. The optimized power consumption and reduction of sensor size are expected to minimize the deployment cost. Future work is going on to develop poor infrastructure and operating cost with better performance.

A few years ago, we would never have imagined an in-depth learning app that includes driverless cars and Alexa, Siri and Google Assistant virtual assistants. But today, these creations are part of our daily lives. DL is captivating us with endless possibilities like fraud detection and pixel recovery.

REFERENCES

1. N.a, Help Net Security, 41.6 Billion IoT Devices will be Generating 79.4 zettabytes of Data in 2025, 2019. Access date: 10 July 2020, Access Link: https://www.helpnetsecurity.com/2019/06/21/connected-iot-devices-forecast/
2. Tabassum, M., & Mathew, K., A Genetic Algorithm Analysis towards Optimization Solutions. Int. J. Digit. Inf. Wireless Commun. (IJDIWC), 4(1), 124–142, 2014.
3. Elijah, O., Rahman, T.A., Orikumhi, I., Leow, C.Y., & Hindia, M.N., An Overview of Internet of Things (IoT) and Data Analytics in Agriculture: Benefits and Challenges. IEEE Internet Things J., 5(5), 3758–3773, 2018.

4. Seth, D., Eswaran, S., Mukherjee, T., & Sachdeva, M. (2020). A Deep Learning Framework for Ensuring Responsible Play in Skill-based Cash Gaming. In 19th IEEE International Conference on Machine Learning and Applications (ICMLA), IEEE, 454–459.

5. Hejazi, H., Rajab, H., Cinkler, T., & Lengyel, L., Survey of Platforms for Massive IoT. In 2018 IEEE International Conference on Future IoT Technologies (Future IoT) (pp. 1–8). IEEE, January, 2018.

6. Tabassum, M., Perumal, S., Mohanan, S., Suresh, P., Cheriyan, S., & Hassan, W., IoT, IR 4.0, and AI Technology Usability and Future Trend Demands: Multi-Criteria Decision-Making for Technology Evaluation. In P. Suresh (ed.), Design Methodologies and Tools for 5G Network Development and Application (pp. 109–144). IGI Global, Hershey, Pennsylvania, USA, 2021.

7. B. Mishra and A. Kertesz, "The Use of MQTT in M2M and IoT Systems: A Survey," in IEEE Access, vol. 8, pp. 201071–201086, 2020, DOI: 10.1109/ACCESS.2020.3035849.

8. AVSYSTEM, Internet of Things, "IoT vs M2M - What Is the Difference?", 2019. Access date: 10 July 2020, Access Link: https://www.avsystem.com/blog/iot-and-m2m-what-is-the-difference/.

9. Fries, J. IoT Agenda, "Why are IoT Developers Confused by MQTT and CoAP?", 2017. Access Date: 19 July 2020, Access Link: https://internetofthingsagenda.techtarget.com/blog/IoT-Agenda/Why-are-IoT-developers-confused-by-MQTT-and-CoAP#:~:text=CoAP%20was%20started%20by%20a,it%20is%20in%20the%20lead.

10. Ubuntupit, M. Top 15 Standard IoT Protocols That You Must Know about, Access Data: 25 June 2020. Access Link: https://www.ubuntupit.com/top-15-standard-iot-protocols-that-you-must-know-about/

11. SpareqEE, "SparqEE CELLv1.0". Access Date: 10 July 2020, Access Link: http://www.sparqee.com/portfolio/sparqee-cell/.

12. Tabassum, M., & Zen, K., Performance Evaluation of ZigBee in Indoor and Outdoor Environment. In 2015 9th International Conference on IT in Asia (CITA) (pp. 1–7). IEEE, August, 2015.

13. Safaei, B., Monazzah, A.M.H., Bafroei, M.B., & Ejlali, A., Reliability Side-effects in Internet of Things Application Layer Protocols. In 2017 2nd International Conference on System Reliability and Safety (ICSRS) (pp. 207–212). IEEE, December, 2017.

14. Sharma, T. & Tabassum, M., Enhanced Algorithm to Optimize QoS and Security Parameters in Ad hoc Networks. In P. Suresh (ed.), Design Methodologies and Tools for 5G Network Development and Application (pp. 1–27). IGI Global, Hershey, Pennsylvania, USA, 2021.

15. IoT-I, Internet of Things Initiative, FP7 EU project, FP7-ICT-2009-5-257565.

16. Scully, P. IOT ANALYTICS, "The Top 10 IoT Segments in 2018 - based on 1,600 real IoT projects", 2018. Access Date: 28 June 2020, Access Link: https://iot-analytics.com/top-10-iot-segments-2018-real-iot-projects/?_scpsug=crawled_5484401_4ca49840-17a8-11e8-854f-f01fafd7b417.

17. Tabassum, M. & Zen, K., Signal Interference Evaluation of Eko Wireless Sensor Network. In 19th International Conference on Transformative Research in Science and Engineering, Business and Social Innovation (SDPS 2014), 2014.

18. Tabassum, M. & Zen, K., Evaluation and Improvement of Data Availability in WSNs Cluster Base Routing Protocol. J. Telecommun. Electron. Comput. Eng. (JTEC), 9(2–9), 111–116, 2017.

19. Tabassum, M., Perumal, S., & Ab Halim, A.H., Review and Evaluation of Data Availability and Network Consistency in Wireless Sensor Networks. Malaysian J. Sci. Health Technol., 4(Special), 56–64, 2019.

20. Brendard, S., Tabassum, M., & Chua, H., Wireless Body Area Networks Channel Decongestion Algorithm. In 2015 9th International Conference on IT in Asia (CITA) (pp. 1–6). IEEE, August, 2015.

21. Chen, S., Gao, X., Wang, J., Xiao, Y., Zhang, Y., & Xu, G., Brand-new Speech Animation Technology based on First Order Motion Model and MelGAN-VC. J. Phys. Conf. Ser., 1828(1), 012029, 2021.

22. Saxena, S. MotionScan: Towards Brain Concussion Detection with a Mobile Tablet Device. 2016.

23. Siarohin, A., Lathuilière, S., Tulyakov, S., Ricci, E., & Sebe, N. First Order Motion Model for Image Animation, 2020. arXiv preprint arXiv:2003.00196.

24. Xue, W., Madonski, R., Lakomy, K., Gao, Z., & Huang, Y. Add-on Module of Active Disturbance Rejection for Set-Point Tracking of Motion Control Systems. IEEE Trans. Ind. Appl., 53, 4028–4040, 2017.

25. Yuehong, Y.I.N., Zeng, Y., Chen, X., & Fan, Y. The Internet of Things in Healthcare: An Overview. J. Indus. Inform. Integ., 1, 3–13, 2016.

26. Li, S., Da Xu, L., & Zhao, S. 5G Internet of Things: A survey. J. Indus. Inform. Integ., 10, 1–9, 2018.

27. Kumar, D.P., Amgoth, T., & Annavarapu, C.S.R. Machine Learning Algorithms for Wireless Sensor Networks: A Survey. Inf. Fusion, 49, 1–25, 2019.

28. Mahdavinejad, M.S., Rezvan, M., Barekatain, M., Adibi, P., Barnaghi, P., & Sheth, A.P. Machine learning for Internet of Things data analysis: A survey. Digit. Commun. Networks, 4(3), 161–175, 2018.

29. Tabassum, M. & Mathew, K. A Genetic Algorithm Analysis Towards Optimization Solutions. Int. J. Digit. Inform. Wireless Commun. (IJDIWC), 4(1), 124–142, 2014.

30. Chang, J.H., Tabassum, M., Qidwai, U., Kashem, S.B.A., Suresh, P., & Saravanakumar, U., Design and Evaluate Low-Cost Wireless Sensor Network Infrastructure to Monitor the Jetty Docking Area in Rural Areas. In Advances in Smart System Technologies (pp. 689–700). Springer, Singapore, 2020.

31. Liang, C.B., Tabassum, M., Kashem, S.B.A., Zama, Z., Suresh, P., & Saravanakumar, U., Smart Home Security System Based on Zigbee. In Advances in Smart System Technologies (pp. 827–836). Springer, Singapore, 2020.

32. Ali, A.B., Tabassum, M., & Mathew, K. A Comparative Study of IGP and EGP Routing Protocols, Performance Evaluation Along Load Balancing and Redundancy Across Different AS. In Proceedings of the International MultiConference of Engineers and Computer Scientists (Vol. 2, pp. 487–967), 2016, March.

5 A Review on Deep Learning Algorithms for Image Processing in Gaming and Animations

Sugandha Chakraverti, Ashish Kumar Chakraverti, Piyush Bhushan Singh, and Rakesh Ranjan

CONTENTS

5.1 Introduction 91
5.2 Machine Learning 92
5.3 Deep Learning..93
    5.3.1 Important Architectures in Deep Learning.......................................94
5.4 Content-Based Gaming Image Retrieval (CBGIR) 94
5.5 Image Classification...95
    5.5.1 Adding Deep Learning to Neural Networks 95
    5.5.2 Benefits of Image Classification 95
    5.5.3 The Image Classification Theory 96
5.6 Image Processing..97
    5.6.1 Point Operations 97
5.7 Image Processing using Deep Learning..98
5.8 Conclusion 99
References...100

5.1 INTRODUCTION

Limited information content or any information that is unilateral yet associated with the most of the images due to the differentiation in focal points when objects appear to be blurred in any of the one image. Most of the cases, images lack valid information or say, they are unilateral with the flow of the content. Multi-modal images are categorized into their several types determined with austere as they reflect diverging information as per the types of images. In case of doctors, for an instance, at times, they find the information too much disintegrated that it results in their misunderstandings. Not only doctors, even several researchers associated in the field of image processing, utilization, and gaming diagnosis found the same problem as well. Throughout the recent years, several researches are continuously assembling with the image processing faculties related to gaming and animation as it still continues

DOI: 10.1201/9781003231530-5

to prove its effectiveness. The image fusion solution automatically detects different types of images along with proper integration of clear images. In short, the image fusion is precisely structured algorithm that combines more than two images to create a new one.

Image fusion is also known for producing multi-modal gaming images that grabbed the attention of a wide range of associated audience and researchers in quiet recent years later categorizing its domain into three potential classes such as DL algorithm, transform domain algorithm, and algorithms for spatial domains. Recently, the focus is majorly on the methods and techniques of DL encouraging scholars from across the globe to conduct DL research even from their comfort zones resulting in image processing and alternatives. Some of the recent analysis on such DL include pixel-level image fusions (steps conclude-training, classification, weight, and fusion), convolutional neural networks (CNN), convolutional sparse representation, stacked auto-encoders (SAEs), and deep Boltzmann machine.

Humans use their vision to collect information that mostly and significantly depends on the image quality. Hence, Spatial resolution such as High-Resolution (HR) is considered much effective for measuring this important attribute because of their plenty delegation, prime features of shooting, and their artificial factors. It is at times quite difficult for the imaging system to receive an information without any interruption, deformity or changes. Therefore, in practical sense, it still remains strictly limited.

Improving the quality of the images is not an easy or inexpensive task. It is quite trending in research and engineering fields related to image sciences. The expensiveness in the field lies in the hardware device practically while approaching toward increasing the superlative image resolutions. In this chapter, we therefore shall also go through the image super-resolution technology used for improving the image quality.

Image super-resolution technology [1] is an image processing approach toward acquiring clear and high-quality images that is believed to be replicated just from the image of a single-frame that is actually structured low resolution (LR). The visual effects of the image get on improving the image super-resolution that is also beneficial during the extraction, recognizing of proper data, traffic, as well as security monitoring.

The deficiency of conventional schematic learning and their over-simplification intensify the image processing information with a rate of higher frequency so that the comparison between the images shall be regenerated using the sporadic practices. This results in DL approaches for melding with the sublimed with resolutions to coherently meliorate the interpretation for reconstructing.

5.2 MACHINE LEARNING

Machine learning is a necessary attribute during the current researches, discoveries, and investigation processes. They are basically used in identifying hidden patterns from the datasets, acquiring of quick and accurate predictions and results, and many other advanced level research programs, just as it goes with the customers. Using machine learning, their preferences can be collected from the pre-existing records equivalent to near interests of other customers [2].

Major studies such as artificial learning, DL, and machine learning has their positions in the areas of computing, real-time imagery, finance, medical science and health, etc. Their urgeness to level up their performance can be broadly seen in open-sourced frameworks during the research methodologies of practical and advanced technologies, with a hope to touch the $24 trillion world market by 2024. Since they find themselves available as well as a necessity in every often field these days, these advanced learning and research are trying their best to reach out to the lowest factor of errors. Therefore, government is discussing broadly to invest more on such advanced learnings so as to be quick with the competitive flow on developing more upon the data-set sectors and research-based dimensions [3].

5.3 DEEP LEARNING

After machine learning, deep learning (DL) technology is used massively in recognizing the patterns and in the areas where there is a conduction of huge image processing. A multi-mode gaming image fusion with DL will be proposed, according to the characters of multi-modal gaming image, gaming diagnostic technology and practical implementation, according to the practical needs for gaming diagnosis. The usage cannot be only seen in MRIs, CT, and SPECT image fusions but also helpful during the issues related to multi-modal gaming image fusions. In addition, the shows the sign of effectiveness in overcoming the limitations of one-page image processing. In order to analyze the performance and stability of the multi-modal gaming images, several experiments are conducted continuously based on visual quality and the various criteria of their quantitative evaluation [4].

Throughout this review, the concentration is greatly upon the applications of DL models that can be used for image processing, but it is quite hard to say how much is the utilization made for the multi-modal batch processing. When compared to the gaming images, the same results may show richness in their clarity. The data quantity of a single image is maximized by the image fusions. Therefore, in this chapter we tried to demonstrate the practical gaming problems, and resolving them, with a tentative research using regulated DL methods.

The introduction of DL model into this chapter is primarily intended so as to develop a new idea of image fusion. Using the practical methodology of DL, we can acquire a new structure that shall become suitable for the fusion for advancing the efficiencies and accuracies resulted from an image processing [5].

DL and neural networks (NN) are the two types of fundamental techniques that are expansively used during classification as well as during prediction processes such as the identification of images and objects, smart homes, automated machines, self-driven cars, etc. Their popularity has risen vastly because they can easily adapt to multiple data types over the domain variants.

DL generally acts as a human brain where it keeps on training a system that refines the data inputs with the help of classification and prediction process, as described above. This filtration process is basically a structure of different active layers where each layer tries to act as a feedback for the adjacent or succeeding layer. There is a continuation in the feedback cycle unless an accurate output i.e., the information, is obtain from the process.

These days, DL techniques are commonly seen taking immeasurable help from artificial neural network during image processing and extraction. Just like DL, NN takes help of CNN for image processing. This CNN is automated in nature and works similar to recurrent neural network (RNN), only exceptional with the fact is the computational language is basically used by the RNN. This RNN therefore uses the concept of feedback loops where the output of one layer is fed as the input of the next layer.

There is hardly any visible limit to the discussions upon DL. DL is used so much these days that it is even used in data processing units. Their active potentiality encourages them to generalize huge data of the smart and metropolitan cities and evaluate them in the areas of gaming and animation. DL in particular aids the faster analysis for rendering an accurate diagnosis. Not only this, the complexity of the health sector is very well managed using DL. This also diagnoses diseases, reduces labor-force, etc. The following section provides an overview of DL applications for gaming image processing [5].

5.3.1 IMPORTANT ARCHITECTURES IN DEEP LEARNING

With the developments of the previous section, much progress was made toward improving the signals, images, videos, and audio processing. Notwithstanding to astray from the topic of discussion, only minute detailing has been added to each section. For more sources, refer to [6–8] and references wherein. Our discussions with be advanced yet short inclusive of some network architectures that we believe had, or will have, an impact on gaming image processing and animation.

Auto encoders use a contracting and an expanding branch for finding the input of a lower dimensionality [9]. They do not require annotations, as the network is trained to predict the original input using loss functions such as $L(\theta)=\| f^{\hat{}}(x)-x\|^2_2$. DL variants use CNN [10], for adding noise to the input [11], or aiming to find the sparse presentations [12].

5.4 CONTENT-BASED GAMING IMAGE RETRIEVAL (CBGIR)

Content-Based Gaming Image Retrieval (CBGIR) is one of the most challenging and ambiguous tasks used to minimize the semantic gap between images and human queries in datasets with rich information content, and to recognize images accurately. The consequences derived from the review goes vivid with ingression for producing convenient yet large balanced datasets for the images. Possibly, there is a shortfall of such datasets in the areas of gaming and animation, even today.

The imbalance gaming image datasets are likely presented by minimizing the semantic gaps that probably evolve between the subordinate features and distinctive semantics, directed by the four-step effective hash code generation techniques. The first stage justifies CNN to be the potent with features so as to withdraw discriminative features such as Fully Connected Layer (FCL) from the images automatically. There is a reduction in the imbalanced dataset within the second stage that makes use of Synthetic Minority Over-sampling Technique (SMOTE). As per the third phase is concerned, we can now clearly see the balanced features practically transmuted to a 13-charactered symbolized code structured from deep SAE. Some of the other relatable dataset experiments are the retrieval performances of the proposed method, error parameter, and the classification performance [13].

Gaming image retrieval research is an aid to radiologists for being beneficial to the usage of gaming and animated images for a long run. This brought advancements to the imaging techniques and automatic diagnosed systems in the medical sector. The gaming images in the modern hospitals store Digital Imaging and Communications in Medicine on text format, for retrieving repositories of the gaming images. Therefore, CBGIR system is actually reliable based on visualizations that always gets itself ready to retrieve continuous and effective gaming images [14].

5.5 IMAGE CLASSIFICATION

Image classification in a computer helps in analyzing the "class" of the images that is exemplified often as an "animal," "plant," "vehicle," etc. With not a big deal, the perfect example fitting to this term is that of Moravec's paradox when it comes to understanding the classification within the machines or various artificial intelligent based learnings.

Image classification in the preliminary stage depended on raw pixel data that broke down the image into individual pixels. As a matter of fact, two different images need not necessarily be alike, even though both of them belong to the same category, because of their feature variants contrast to each other. This, thus, brought challenges to the computers for effective visualization and categorization of the images [15].

5.5.1 ADDING DEEP LEARNING TO NEURAL NETWORKS

DL is a type of machine learning as well as a segment to the artificial intelligence (AI). Such advanced learning is altogether advantageous with NN for allowing the machines to read the given data. While advanced with the NN, data is input through the node layers for communicating the results to the next node layer. This process is continued until the machine reaches the output layer, and provides a concrete answer.

There are various types of NN among which the CNN are mostly associated with DL during the process of image classification. In CNNs, the nodes in the hidden layers don't always share their output with every node in the next layer (known as convolutional layers) (Figure 5.1). DL allows machines to identify and extract features from images, furthermore, aiding programmers to hardly enter into the filters manually.

5.5.2 BENEFITS OF IMAGE CLASSIFICATION

Image classification are potentially active in vast yet reliable growths. For instance, the self-driving cars (Figure 5.2) make use of the image classification for identifying their surrounding objects such as trees, people, traffic lights, etc.

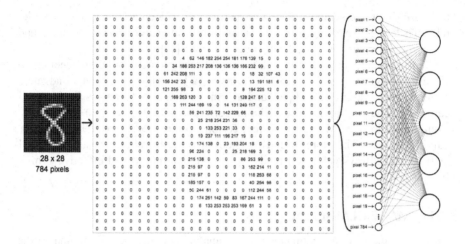

FIGURE 5.1   Computer "vision" via data. (Source: KDnuggets.)

FIGURE 5.2   Classification of object detection, here, the self-driving car.

Image classification also helps in analyzing the gaming images. It is also used in suggesting and depicting any traces of illness in the human body. Other usages include proper organization of several types of photo collections.

5.5.3   THE IMAGE CLASSIFICATION THEORY

Not only humans and creatures, computers have visions too. A vision that can classify any object just upon seeing a particular image. Today, the pervasiveness of image classification is in a good shape because of the utilization of DL in the curriculum of image processing. This advancement also resulted in the involvement of the CNNs coinciding with strong exploration.

Image classification is a definitive learning for targeting set of classes and recognizing them with proper set of exemplified images. In such classification process,

CNN regards the raw pixel data as an input for extracting the necessary features from a particular image such as textures and shapes. This way the CNNs extract the contents from the image successfully. The input image of a CNN has dimensions W×H×C, where W and H are the width and height of the image in pixels, respectively, and C is the number of images color channels.

Generally, CNN constitutes of stack modules known to perform three operations. They are the Convolution, Rectified Linear Unit (ReLU), and Pooling. Convolution helps CNN in creating a filter map for the input image. ReLU brings non-linearity into the model whereas Pooling acts helpful in the reduction of the dimensions of the feature map. When the obtained feature map is shaped once again into a long vector, many connected layers are used in the place for completing the final task with the help of Softmax activation function. The output derived from this function is valued between 0 and 1. In this review, any image processing method that takes the Softmax activation function and modifies it compared to baseline methods is considered as a "post-processing" technique [16].

It is basically the accurate calculations that measures the performance of deep networks in the subject of image classification. The calculation is such that the ratio between the correctly classified images and the aggregate quantity of images defines how metric they are in solving the tasks of CNN in gaming imaging such as patch-based classification processes [17].

5.6 IMAGE PROCESSING

Image processing is an operation that begins with one grey scale or colored image (images with an array of pixels) and ends or returns with the other one. Throughout this chapter, we are explaining certain techniques useful for operating the grey-scale images in order to locate their features edges. The derived result is such that there is an equal quantity of pixels as well as grey levels. The resulting image with this similar size is presented with modified brightness with the help of the spatial relationship to many other pixels. This thus, produces a new image. Depending on what is considered to be of an absolute interest, the image is processed and modified intentionally to emphasize the original one. With the resulted and desired features such as objects, edges, boundaries, etc., the image later goes through under operation for extract the background (i.e., uninteresting) data from that particular image for isolating other additional information.

5.6.1 Point Operations

Each pixel value when replaced by a new one that is wholly and solely dependable on the original value gives an idea of a simple methodology. Thus, this is definitely known as a "point" operation keeping it distanced from other operations such as "neighborhood" and "global." In particular, if we carefully examine the original brightness that is covered with a small fraction of the total range, new values are seen increasing the contrast of the image. This is called "Point Transformation." The relationship between original and replacement brightness values is often called a transfer function, and can alter the appearance of an image as in Figure 5.3.

FIGURE 5.3 Examples of different transfer functions applied to an image: (a) original, (b) logarithmic, (c) histogram equalization, and (d) negative.

The given functions don't necessarily need to be a linear. Logarithmic function is a type of function that imitates the works of photography. This thus gives the function an inclined slop for semi-log plotting which is also known as the "gamma" value. Its positive values try to constrict the brightness displayed on the end range whenever it expands to the darker segments. Negative transfer functions are also often used for reversing the contrast of the image. Histogram equalization method is a type of non-linear transfer function useful for particular images where pixels of a proportionate value consist of particular grey shades.

Transfer function derives its shape from the brightness histogram of the original image in higher gradients so that the details are much clear to observe. It is mostly used in the display devices and are often monotonic. It also grants permission for inserting grey level variants for deriving good output. This causes the values to become unconvinced and cynical about either accepting the minimized or the maximized ones. Brightness gradients are visualized in hegemony settling the brightest pixels into extreme bright or dark values. The result is to superimpose brightness contour lines on the image. No other techniques are so impactful upon transforming the original image. Indeed, with many modern systems it is not even necessary to operate on the image itself to produce the transformation.

Look Up Tables or LUTs are non-destructive and quick-witted methods for executing the transfer functions. With the help of this method, the function is known to produce the display and keep the video output under-control. Thus, it is very convenient to change the façade of the display.

5.7 IMAGE PROCESSING USING DEEP LEARNING

Image processing plays an important role in the fields like image mining, gaming imaging, gaming image processing, web mining etc. It is also the Content-Based Gaming Image Retrieval (CBGIR) system that is quick enough for retrieving the gaming images. This chapter on image processing and segmentation is deep with AI type DL. Its recapitulation presents several possible advantages for using DL methods into gaming and image mining. It also throws an insight of content-based image retrieval and identifying a flaw in the gaming image.

Besides optical sensing and image capturing systems [18], process images are the new standpoints for process monitoring. When these process images are put to use, the Deep Belief Network (DBN) are directly manipulated into the existing networks for extracting the features from those images and detect the scheduled faults. Meanwhile, the sub-networks are operated to extracting the local features from the sub-images. The global network exceptionally extracts and improves the training efficiency without deteriorating the fault detection accuracy. On release, a new statistic is further developed in the course of the framework customized for DL [19].

As much as the current AI techniques are concerned, DL techniques are the most stabilized variables in the health, infrastructure, research, gaming, and UI/UX sectors. Their available is widespread rapidly each passing day because of its effective and accurate results. They also aid in the implicit abilities of engineering workshops, integrational ability for embedding words, and again an ability for dealing with complex and unstructured dataset. Beyond this, the concept is also related digital texts in electronic health records (EHRs), clinical texts on social media, text in electronic gaming reports and gaming images. On the growing popularity of DL and its algorithms, the responsibility toward several domains have risen as well. It is very well observed in the 2017–2020 reports [20], where the 2019 report stated the publication up to 4 times, that is more than the year 2018. Growths are seen increasing rapidly after the learning acted even in the gaming techniques and animating applications for image processing [20].

5.8 CONCLUSION

The technical translation of DL methods in image processing is still in the juvenile phase. These techniques have grown vigorously useful in tackling with the tasks conducting image processing and yet stay aback at times due to certain limitations. Since there was a deficiency in the exclusiveness of the annotated experimental data, the researchers adjusted to the utilization of simulated data only, validating hardly any proposed techniques to run it on a large-scale. This chapter discusses the challenges for clinical translations used for DL methods in image processing by concluding and summarizing the major key findings on processing images in different aspects. Wilson et al. [21] examined the challenges and issues faced during the clinical translation using the techniques of spectroscopic optical imaging. This prepared a broader space for us to focus more on the upcoming hurdles impending while translating imaging modalities. Therefore, this thesis particularly concentrates on the facilitations made by the DL application while integrating the approaches of image processing.

At last, reviewing this chapter shows that the methods used for DL is prominently utilized in the field of personal activity intelligence (PAI), CBGIR, etc., for simplifying extensive number of translations that would go on a long term. Therefore, with the help of several studies, research, and investigation, we analyzed that even these minimalistic studies on image processing are some of the little concerns for contributing to the bigger picture challenges to what we call it as the future open challenges associated to the applications on DL such as detecting problems in optical inversion, image post-processing, and annotation on semantic imaging.

REFERENCES

1. Zhang J., Shao, M., Yu, L., and Li, Y., Image Super-Resolution Reconstruction Based on Sparse Representation and Deep Learning, Signal Process. Image Commun., 87, 115925, September 2020.
2. Arunakranthi, G., Rajkumar, B., Chandra, V., Rao, S., and Harshvardhan, A., Advanced Patterns of Predictions and Cavernous Data Analytics Using Quantum Machine Learning, Mater. Today Proc., 2021.
3. Raju, B., and Bonagiri, R., A Cavernous Analytics Using Advanced Machine Learning for Real World Datasets in Research Implementations, Mater. Today Proc., 2021.
4. Li, Y., Zhao, J., and Zhihan, Lv., Li, J., Medical Image Fusion Method by Deep Learning, Int. J. Cogn. Comput. Eng., 2, June 2021, 21-29.
5. Bhattacharyaa, S., Reddy Maddikuntaa, P.K., VietPhamb, Q., Gadekallu, T.R., Krishnan, S.R., Chowdhary, C.L., and MamounAlazab, Md. J.P., Deep Learning and Medical Image Processing for Coronavirus (COVID-19) Pandemic: A Survey, Sustain. Cities Soc., 65, 102589, February 2021.
6. Benjio, Y., Courville, A., and Vincent, P., Representation Learning: A Review and New Perspectives, IEEE Trans. Pattern Anal. Mach. Intell., 35, 1798–1828, 2013.
7. Goodfellow, I., Bengio, Y., Courville, A., and Bengio, Y., Deep Learning, vol. 1, MIT Press, Cambridge, 2016.
8. Litjens, G., Kooi, T., Bejnordi, B.E., Setio, A.A.A., Ciompi, F., Ghafoorian, M., et al., A Survey on Deep Learning in Medical Image Analysis, Med. Image Anal., 42, 60–88, 2017.
9. Vincent, P., Larochelle, H., Bengio, Y., and Manzagol, P.-A., Extracting and Composing Robust Features with Denoising Autoencoders, Proc. 25th Int. Conf. Machine Learning, ACM, 1096–1103, 2008.
10. Holden, D., Saito, J., Komura, T., and Joyce, T., Learning Motion Manifolds with Convolutional Autoencoders, SIGGRAPH Asia 2015 Technical Briefs, ACM, 1–4. November 2015 Article No.: 18. https://doi.org/10.1145/2820903.2820918.
11. Vincent, P., Larochelle, H., Lajoie, I., Bengio, Y., and Manzagol, P.-A., Stacked Denoising Autoencoders: Learning Useful Representations in a Deep Network with a Local Denoising Criterion, J. Mach. Learn. Res., 11, 3371–3408, 2010.
12. Huang, F.J., Boureau, Y.-L., LeCun, Y., Huang, F.J., Boureau, Y.-L., LeCun, Y., et al., Unsupervised Learning of Invariant Feature Hierarchies with Applications to Object Recognition, IEEE Conf. Comput. Vision Pattern Recog., 2007. CVPR'07, IEEE, 1–8, 2007.
13. Ozturk, S., Stacked Auto-Encoder Based Tagging with Deep Features for Content-Based Medical Image Retrieval, Expert Systems Appl., 161, 113693, 2020.
14. Shamna, P., Govindan, V.K., and Abdul Nazeer, K.A., Content-Based Medical Image Retrieval by Spatial Matching of Visual Words, J. King Saud Univ. Comput. Inf. Sci., 2018. https://doi.org/10.1016/j.jksuci.2018.10.002
15. https://www.thinkautomation.com/eli5/eli5-what-is-image-classification-in-deep-learning/
16. Salvi, M.,Acharya, U.R., Molinari, F., and Meiburger, K.M., The Impact of Pre- and Post-Image Processing Techniques on Deep Learning Frameworks: A Comprehensive Review for Digital Pathology Image Analysis, Comput. Biol. Medicine, 128, 104129, January 2021.

17. Y. LeChun, Y., Bengio, Y., and Hinton, G., Deep Learning, Nature, 521, 436–444, 2015.
18. Karanam, S.R., Shrinivas, Y., and Vamshi Krishna, M., Study on Image Processing Using Deep Learning Techniques, Mater. Today Proc., 2020.
19. Lyu, Y., Chen, J., and Song, Y., Image-Based Process Monitoring Using Deep Learning Framework, Chemom. Intell. Lab. Syst., 189, 8–17, 2019.
20. Pandey, B., Pandey, D.K., Mishra, B.P., and Rhmann, W., A Comprehensive Survey of Deep Learning in the field of Medical Imaging and Medical Natural Language Processing: Challenges and Research Directions, J. King Saud. Univ. Comput. Inf. Sci., 29 January, 2021.
21. Wilson, B.C., Jermyn, M., and Leblond, F., Challenges and Opportunities in Clinical Translation of Biomedical Optical Spectroscopy and Imaging, J. Biomed. Opt., 23(3),1–13, 2018. doi: 10.1117/1.JBO.23.3.030901. PMID: 29512358; PMCID: PMC5838403.

6 Artificial Intelligence in Games

Transforming the Gaming Skills

Abhisht Joshi, Moolchand Sharma, and
Jafar Al Zubi

CONTENTS

6.1 Introduction 103
    6.1.2 How will AI Reinvent the Experience of Gaming?........................ 106
        6.1.2.1 Advantages of AI in Gaming... 106
6.2 Gaming Experience 107
    6.2.1 Power of Voice in Gaming.. 107
    6.2.2 Real Gaming Experience to Players 108
        6.2.2.1 Three-Dimensional Visualization Techniques 108
        6.2.2.2 Simulation Based on Physics 108
        6.2.2.3 Virtual Reality 109
        6.2.2.4 Augmented Reality 110
        6.2.2.5 Extended Reality.. 110
    6.2.3 Necessity of RL for Adaptability in Games 112
    6.2.4 In-Game Support to Players by AI Powered Chatbots.................... 113
    6.2.5 Gives an Overall Ultimate Gaming Experience.............................. 114
6.3 Early Game AI vs Complex Game AI... 115
    6.3.1 Early Game AI.. 115
    6.3.2 Complex Game AI.. 115
    6.3.3 Video Game AI... 116
        6.3.3.1 Finite State Machines 116
        6.3.3.2 Path-Finding.. 117
        6.3.3.3 Real-Time Play Complex AI... 118
6.4 Conclusion and Future Scope 119
References... 120

6.1 INTRODUCTION

It is important to consider the past and present before embarking on future game production. In October 1958, the game design and production began. William Higinbotham, an American physicist, created the first video game. It was an old tennis game known as "Pong" that was very common at the time. Since then, the number of games, video game platforms, and game types has increased dramatically. As a result, many people showed a willingness to play, and many people took it out on them. The gaming industry has evolved rapidly because of significant advancements in hardware and design and development strategies. Artificial Intelligence (AI) has aided the expansion by improving the gaming experience. In addition, it has piqued players' attention by exceeding their standards for the game. AI software improves creation processes such as image production, animation generation, improving the performance of non-player characters (NPCs), story layers, characterization, and graphics authenticity.

When you talk about AI, you are talking about computers that mimic the human mind. The primary goal of AI in gaming is to make games smarter. It gives the games a natural system to support NPCs' intelligent actions. AI offers intelligent game controls that allow for clever character communication and movement. To put it another way, AI brings the game closer to reality. It investigates the dynamic relationships between agents and game environments in general. Various games provide agents with fascinating and complex problems to solve, making video games ideal for AI study and studying how to use AI technologies to achieve human-level success.

In contrast, playing games is known as AI in the gaming experience. It investigates the dynamic relationships between agents and game environments in general. Various games provide agents with fascinating and complex problems to solve, making video games ideal for AI study. These virtual worlds are safe and manageable. Furthermore, these game environments have an endless supply of data for machine learning (ML) algorithms and are much faster than in real-time. Because of these characteristics, games are a particular and common domain for AI study. On the other hand, AI has aided games in being better in terms of how we play, understand, and style them [1].

In general, game AI is concerned with perception and decision-making in virtual environments. There are some significant challenges and solutions associated with these components. The primary challenge is that, particularly in strategic games, the state space of the sport is extremely broad. The entire framework has effectively modeled large-scale state-space with deep neural networks as representation learning has increased. The second issue is that it is difficult to learn proper policies for making decisions in a dynamic, unknown environment. Data-driven approaches such as supervised learning and reinforcement learning (RL) are viable solutions for this issue. The third issue is that the vast majority of game AI is created in a controlled virtual world. Therefore, the ability of AI to be transferred between games could be a major challenge. To address this issue, a more generalized learning system is also required. Hence, if we talk about AI in gaming detail, there are two types of game AI techniques: deterministic and non-deterministic [2, 3].

i. **Deterministic:** Deterministic performance or action is predetermined and predictable. There is not any ambiguity. A simple chasing algorithm is an example of deterministic action. By advancing along the x and y coordinate axes until the character's x and y coordinates coincide with the target position, you can specifically code an NPC to travel toward a target point.

ii. **Nondeterministic:** The opposite of deterministic behavior is non-deterministic behavior. There is a degree of ambiguity in behavior, and it is very unpredictable (the degree of uncertainty depends on the AI method employed and how well that method is understood). An NPC learning to adapt to a player's combat strategies is an example of non-deterministic actions. A neural network, a Bayesian method, or a genetic algorithm may be used in this form of learning.

The bread and butter of game AI are deterministic AI techniques. These techniques are easy to implement, understand, test, and debug because they are predictable, fast, and simple. Despite their many advantages, deterministic methods predict all scenarios and code all actions on the developers' shoulders. Furthermore, deterministic approaches obstruct learning and evolution. Deterministic habits begin to become predictable after a little practice. This, in a sense, shortens a game's lifespan.

On the other hand, learning and volatile gameplay are made easier with non-deterministic methods. Furthermore, developers are not required to code all actions directly in advance of all potential scenarios. Non-deterministic approaches can also learn and extrapolate independently and foster emergent behavior, which occurs without clear instructions.

However, if we considered ML methods, RL has been commonly used for a long time to solve these problems. In recent years, deep learning (DL) has achieved impressive success in computer vision and natural language processing (NLP) [4]. As a result, many video games with deep reinforcement learning (DRL) have achieved performance beyond human ability. At the same time, there are still some challenges in this domain that need to be tackled.

The gaming industry worldwide has values of around $109+ billion, making this industry one of the central points to perform research and thus improve its performance by integrating it with AI, specifically DL. Figure 6.1 shows the gaming industry size as compared to other industries. Most gamers do not consider gaming as a sector, but it is becoming such a large and influential entertainment industry that it attracts an increasing number of professionals. We must first dismantle the gaming value chain. Game engines, which game engine owners normally license, are used to

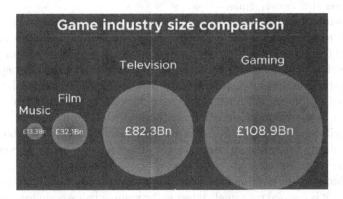

FIGURE 6.1 Comparison of gaming industry size with other industries.

create games. These game creators then depend on publishers to bring their creations to life [4].

6.1.2 How will AI Reinvent the Experience of Gaming?

With AI changing the landscape of gaming, we are revolutionizing the gaming industry with captivating gaming experiences that cannot be achieved on any other platforms.

Jefferson Valadares, CEO, Doppio Games

AI has shown positive results in the gaming industry since its inception. In every aspect of the gaming industry, AI has always been the same. It not only learned to play chess, but it also defeated some of the best players in the world. Furthermore, gaming companies are now employing AI in a more dynamic setback process, such as determining the main AI benefits in games.

6.1.2.1 Advantages of AI in Gaming

The major advantages of AI in gaming are as follows:

- **Creating a real gaming experience:** A player will normally play a game if they can relate to it; the more authentic the experience, the more the player will find it enjoyable and worthwhile to play. As ML and DL become more mainstream, more progress is made in these fields. As a result, the gaming experience matters a lot and AI has emerged as one of the major factors leading to a better gaming experience.
- **Improves the experience of audio and video:** There are two ways a game communicates with the player: audio and video; if both are not of high quality, the player is more likely to dislike the game. Thus, image and audio auto-regeneration are promising ML technology for real-time communications. Furthermore, the algorithms can produce higher-quality images from lower-quality images. ML algorithms can also detect and suppress loud noises produced in the background that are unintelligible and unimportant during your conversation.
- **Identification of bugs:** The ubiquitous restricted random/coverage-oriented verification technology, or structured verification technology, is used in today's bug-finding approaches. However, as designs become more complex, new methodologies and methods are needed to ensure long-term quality. This can range from AI and ML to upgrading methodologies to provide more automation and less error tracking in a notebook or spreadsheet. If the AI model is correctly and appropriately trained, it will assist in identifying bugs and removing them immediately. This area is growing in popularity because it saves developers from having to hardcode bug fixes every time.
- **Enhancing the gaming experience and many more:** Though AI is widely used, it is focused on a single target in the gaming industry: to have a better gaming experience. While there is still much improvement in AI in gaming,

there is much substantial advancement going on right now. Day by day, progress is made in this area, and improvisation and technology updates occur.

6.2 GAMING EXPERIENCE

As the name suggests, the gaming experience means how the player feels the game every time they play it. Therefore, the gaming experience depends upon the following factors:

- **Interaction with the player:** Certain games necessitate live interaction with a live player, while others necessitate interaction with an in-game character; the more interaction, the better the gaming experience.
- **Audio capability and quality of graphics:** Audio and graphic quality connect with the gamer and provide the actual gaming experience. This is the most important factor of the gaming experience as the more it is better, the user will find it real, and the gamer will be able to believe that he is actually in the game.
- **Degree of difficulty:** Even though every game gives the player the option to choose the difficulty level before starting the game, developers must bear in mind that the game should not be too difficult for the player to leave, nor should it be too straightforward for the game to end in a few hours.
- **The level of intelligence in-game characters:** Every player's intelligence is important because they are the ones who will lead the game to its conclusion; if they are not properly qualified, the game will be stuck indefinitely. NPC intelligence is also essential, as NPCs cannot simply be programmed to do anything they want, as this would seem strange. As a result, the NPC's intelligence level is also significant.

AI is focusing on the variables mentioned above to have a superior gaming experience. In addition, AI assists game developers in improving the gaming experience on mobile devices and other platforms. The five ways to use AI to redefine the ultimate gaming experience are as follows:

1. Power of voice in gaming
2. Real gaming experiences to players
3. The necessity of RL for adaptability in games
4. In-game support to players by AI-powered chatbots
5. The overall ultimate experience of gaming

6.2.1 POWER OF VOICE IN GAMING

The way games are played changing thanks to AI-based voice intelligence. The term "AI" sounds more rational now than at any other time in gaming history. This also contributed to a more realistic gaming experience. Additionally, voice-controlled games allow players to use voice commands to control the game. This results in a more enjoyable gaming experience. When playing these games, players will simply tell their characters what to do. For example, gamers may use simple verbal commands to tell their game characters to run, swim, jump, hide, open the door, change weapons, and do something else. Since voice commands save them from remembering various keys and their variations, they can provide a more smooth and realistic gaming experience. In contrast to buttons or keys, using voice commands is a more natural process.

The following are some examples of voice-controlled AI games:

a. Bot Colony
b. Broken Seal
c. The 3% Challenge
d. Westworld: The Maze
e. LEGO: Duplo Stories

The accent problem is a major issue in this type of game; various world regions have different accents, which confuse AI games because the user has to repeat the command repeatedly, resulting in poor game results. Since AI-created voice sounds natural, and the voice generated also plays a crucial role in making it more realistic, voice AI can make the game more interactive. AI provides digitally created voices, and its ability to initiate interactions through dialogues aids players in completing several tasks and more. Voice AI has only recently started to reshape the gaming industry. Voice AI has limitless potential, but it also creates a customized and dynamic gaming experience for gamers. There is still much progress in voice AI, and definitive research is being conducted to improve the current voice AI. Scientists and game developers are collaborating to improve its accuracy [5, 6].

6.2.2 REAL GAMING EXPERIENCE TO PLAYERS

The hyper-realistic gaming experience is another advantage of AI in gaming. AI brought the following changes in creating realistic gaming experiences.

6.2.2.1 Three-Dimensional Visualization Techniques

The realism of three-dimensional (3D) visualization in simulation software is getting better. Although most simulation packages had two-dimensional (2D) visualization featured ten years ago, most now have 3D visualization features. The simulation techniques used, however, do not provide a realistic representation of the virtual world. To improve the quality of 3D visualizations, we should look to the video game industry for research solutions and avoid hardcoding wherever possible. Furthermore, since these games' common special effect techniques are implemented in various open-source and commercial game engines, they can be modified and reused in other areas [7].

6.2.2.2 Simulation Based on Physics

Since a game created with AI will be trained on many data, it will have a greater understanding of physics as it will be fed with the data following physics laws,

FIGURE 6.2 Making AI model to adapt the physics laws.

making the AI model adapt to physics law, making it to be real so the player can relate game with real-life making the gaming experience more real as shown in Figure 6.2.

6.2.2.3 Virtual Reality

Virtual reality, also known as VR, is a computer-generated simulation. A person can interact with an artificial 3D world using electronic devices such as special goggles with a screen or sensors-equipped gloves [8]. Anyone with these devices will enjoy the unique VR experience depicted in Figure 6.3.

FIGURE 6.3 Unique experience of VR.

FIGURE 6.4   AR used in *Pokémon Go*.

6.2.2.4 Augmented Reality

Augmented reality (AR) is an immersive experience of a real-world environment. Computer-generated perceptual knowledge is used to improve the objects in the real world, often through several sensory modalities such as visual, auditory, haptic, somatosensory, and olfactory. Figure 6.4 depicts AR in the famous game Pokémon Go, while Figure 6.5 depicts the distinction between AR and VR.

6.2.2.5 Extended Reality

Extended reality (XR) refers to all real-and-virtual collaborative environments and human-machine interactions generated by computer technology and wearables. The

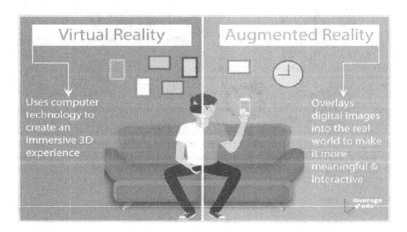

FIGURE 6.5   AR vs. VR.

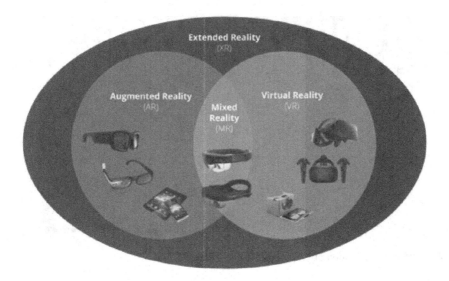

FIGURE 6.6 Extend reality with AR, MR, and VR.

"X" represents a variable for any current or future spatial computing technologies. Figure 6.6 depicts a clearer picture of the XR.

Games today are intelligent and visually pleasing in ways that were unimaginable 10–15 years ago. Figure 6.7 shows the evolution of game characters, and Figure 6.8 shows an example of the evolution of graphics in games over the years.

The definition of gaming has changed thanks to AR. The VR game "Pokémon Go" is a well-known example. Another example is "Until you fall," a VR sword combat game depicted. One of the most common problems with video games is that items look fine from afar, but as you get closer to take a closer look, objects

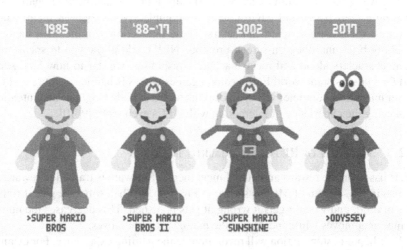

FIGURE 6.7 Evolution of game characters.

FIGURE 6.8   Evolution of graphics in *Need for Speed.*

make poorly and become pixelated, resulting in bad game quality. NVidia and Microsoft are cooperating to solve this issue by investing in DL to improve rendering. Computer vision and DL algorithms can help with the dynamic representation of finer details, a problem in the past. Algorithms acting as NPCs are another significant factor contributing to improving the real-world gaming experience. AI-based NPCs allow you to play against less predictable opponents. These adversaries may also change their difficulty level based on the user. As a player learns how to play the game, the enemies may become smarter and react to the user in specific ways that the user has never seen before based on the user's behavior. Companies are developing NPCs by using data from top players as training data, allowing for better and quicker reinforcement training.

The way players communicate with friendly NPCs is another big challenge in creating a realistic virtual environment. To complete your goals in many games, you must speak with scripted characters. These interactions, on the other hand, are normally brief and obey on-screen prompts. NLP could allow you to speak to in-game characters aloud and receive accurate responses, similar to how Siri, Alexa, and Google Assistant work. Furthermore, games with VR haptics or imaging of the player may allow computer vision algorithms to detect body language and intentions, enhancing the experience of interacting with NPCs even more [9, 10].

6.2.3   Necessity of RL for Adaptability in Games

RL is based on the reward and punishment theory. Software is trained to reward and punish in RL, a form of ML, as shown in Figure 6.9. When software gets it right, it gets praised, and when it gets it wrong, it gets punished. This decreases the number of incorrect moves while increasing the number of right moves.

RL's hyper customization will revolutionize the gaming experience. For example, RL determines the player's skill level, and the strategy or strategies are adjusted accordingly [11]. To better grasp the application of AI in the gaming room, consider

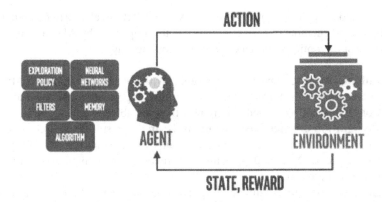

FIGURE 6.9 Reinforcement learning.

Deep Mind's Alpha Zero. Alpha Zero is a program that aims to understand the recurring patterns and properties of games, such as board symmetry.

This is possible, thanks to a new type of RL in which *AlphaGo Zero* serves as its instructor. The software begins with an untrained artificial neural network that has no prior knowledge of Go. Then, combining this neural network with a strong search algorithm, the program plays the game against itself. Finally, the neural network is trained and tuned to anticipate m as it plays. Figure 6.10 shows the Alpha Go Zero beating Ke Jei.

6.2.4 In-Game Support to Players by AI Powered Chatbots

AI-powered chatbots benefit both game developers and players by offering the best in-game support. These chatbots can apply ML algorithms to implement human-level

FIGURE 6.10 AlphaGo Zero beating Ke Jei.

reasoning and logic for efficient gameplay. VR and XR are also driving up demand for AI-powered chatbots like never before. Chatbots operated by AI contribute to the improvement of gaming experiences in the following ways:

- **Enhancement to players' interactions:** With the aid of chatbots, real-time interactions with players make the gaming experience more interactive. Conversational AI is used to empower these chatbots.
- **Recognition of voice-based commands:** In contrast to text-based or key-based commands, voice-based commands are the more natural way to communicate. NLP and speech-to-text recognition technologies are used to allow these commands.
- **Enhancement to customer support:** The new generation is enthralled with video games, with gamers playing them at all hours of the day and night. As a result of this zeal, assistance is needed immediately, regardless of the time. AI-powered chatbots improve customer service by offering in-game support 24 hours a day, seven days a week, at lower operating costs.

6.2.5 GIVES AN OVERALL ULTIMATE GAMING EXPERIENCE

When playing a game, gamers pay close attention to every detail. Gamers evaluate the gaming experience not only in terms of visual appeal or graphic quality but also in terms of how realistic and related the game is. The game is evaluated in every way possible. AI plays a critical role in elevating the gaming experience. The in-game experience of a player is first decoded in order to improve it. Developers use ML algorithms such as SVM or neural networks to decode the data. As in the *AlphaGo Zero* game, models of game player experience are developed. For data preparation, the game's specific pattern and details of game-player interaction are needed. Data may be collected using a variety of methods, such as a questionnaire or a survey. Since each player reacts differently to various scenarios, hardcoding a common algorithm is difficult; this is where ML and DL come into play [2, 12].

Several other tech firms, including Facebook, have been focusing on AI in gaming. For example, Facebook's new AI will remove characters from YouTube videos for a better gaming experience. In addition, the Facebook Research team has developed *Vid2Game*, an AI that will allow playable characters to be extracted from real people's images. It is a more advanced variant of the 1980s' full-motion video (FMV) games. The Facebook Game Development team used two neural networks, Pose2Pose and Pose2Frame. The video was fed into the Pose2Pose neural network in the first level, designed for specific actions such as dancing, tennis, and fencing. The system recognizes and separates the individual from their surroundings, isolating him and his pose. Pose2Frame then inserts the individual and their movements and whatever object they are carrying into a new scene with small artifacts in the second stage. The character's action is then controlled using a joystick or keyboard.

A few short videos were used in the system's training to analyze events such as fencing, dancing, and tennis. It was able to screen out unwanted people and integrate various camera angles. This research is like Adobe Premiere Pro's "content-aware fill" function, which uses AI to remove different elements from video. NVIDIA and a few other companies have also worked on AI to convert real-world videos into virtual worlds, making it ideal for video games [13].

6.3 EARLY GAME AI VS COMPLEX GAME AI

AI has been used in a variety of games in recent years, ranging from modern real-time strategy games like *StarCraft II* to classic games like *checkers*. As a result, AI and ML have a long background in game evolution. The development of virtual worlds in video games has proven to be a useful test-bed for AI algorithms. Using AI in games is also a good idea.

6.3.1 EARLY GAME AI

The first known example of AI in gaming was inspired as a demonstration of computing at the Festival of Britain in 1950. In 1951, Ferranti introduced a custom-built Nimrod machine, which used the Nim game to demonstrate its mathematical potential. *Nim* is a two-player game where players take turns by removing one to three items from the pile. On the contrary, the player who re-enters the game is the one who re-enters the game. Although Nimrod was created to play Nim, Ferranti thought that creating a computer that would play a complex game would also solve complex problems. As a result, Nimrod had no program. Instead, it had a set of complex hard-wired collections of logic to follow. Thus, Nimrod did not have traditional AI, but its ability to play Nim made it competitive, surprising, and intimidating players alike.

6.3.2 COMPLEX GAME AI

Arthur Samuel of the tech giant IBM introduced one of the first applications to learn about conventional ML in sports (who coined the term "machine learning"). Samuel accepted the challenge of the game checkers in 1956, which required both easy play and complex strategy. His work on the first commercial computer, the scientific IBM 701, resulted in the development of two key principles in ML. The invention of alpha-beta pruning was the first.

"Do not take the time to see how bad an idea is if it is undeniably awful," Patrick Winston said of the basic definition of alpha-beta. The Minimax algorithm is used to reduce the number of nodes that must be evaluated inside a tree—in this case, for two-player games—and alpha-beta pruning is a tree-search optimization technique. In a nutshell, when the machine chooses a move, it is represented as a game state space tree, with each level representing the computer or player's next move. The Minimax algorithm aims to optimize the smallest benefit possible. Alpha-beta prunes parts of the tree that don't improve a player's reward out of the evaluation; only the middle move can help player X win (assuming that both players will be playing optimally), shown in Figure 6.11.

Samuel's second central idea was the combination of self-play and rote learning. Samuel pitted his software against itself to enhance its efficiency, as well as remembering each move it had experienced (dutifully recorded on magnetic tape), as well as its terminal "reward" value. His software was a *checkers* game for amateurs, but it incorporated ideas that are still used today. For example, the alpha-beta search

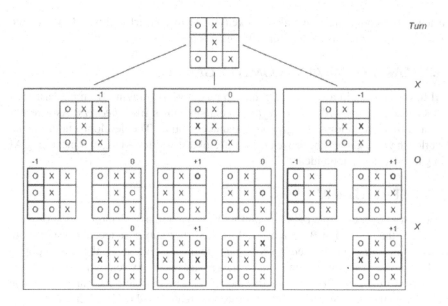

FIGURE 6.11 Minimax tree for Tic-Tac-Toe.

method was revived in the game of chess 40 years later. Garry Kasparov, a chess grandmaster, was defeated by IBM's Deep Blue in 1996. Deep Blue ran simultaneous game-state tree search, pruned with alpha-beta pruning, to speed up the process of calculating the computer's next step (by searching 200 million positions per second and decide up to 20 moves for the future). In 2015, Google used DL (neural networks) for move selection and Monte Carlo search for applying previously learned moves to the game of Go. In 2015, AlphaGo defeated a professional human player, and in 2017, it defeated the world's top player. AlphaGo reapplied Self-play (which was developed by Samuel for checkers approximately 60 years ago) to improve its play and store the moves that were previously known.

6.3.3 VIDEO GAME AI

Early video games had no idea that instead of relying on state machines to predict movement, their rivals used AI (such as in Space Invaders). Pac-Man raised the difficulty of the enemy in 1980 to aid the player in path-finding (or away from the player in the case of escape). Furthermore, each opponent had a distinct personality, making the game more unpredictable.

Let us look at some of the current methods in video games.

6.3.3.1 Finite State Machines

Though not technically AI, finite state machines (FSMs) have long been a part of games, providing the foundation for what appears to be intelligent actions. An FSM is a computation model that allows states to change in response to external input. FSMs have differing behaviors for game entities in the context of games. For example,

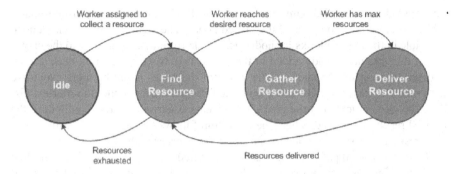

FIGURE 6.12   The finite state machine for a real time strategy worker NPC.

Figure 6.12 depicts an NPC to whom the player can delegate a role. Once delegated, the NPC performs the task based on the various behaviors required to complete it.

The FSM in Figure 6.12 depicts a worker NPC who is tasked with collecting resources by the player. Following its assignment, the NPC locates the desired resource, collects it, and transports it to a collection point. This cycle repeats until all resources have been depleted, at which point the NPC will become idle.

6.3.3.2 Path-Finding

In games, the ability to navigate in their surroundings by the NPCs is a common feature. Path-finding is a term used to describe an ability that can be learned in several ways. One of the most well-known is A. The A algorithm is a variant of Dijkstra's shortest path algorithm, in which NPC destinations are represented as the nodes of a graph (see Figure 6.13). There are two types of lists that A* can deal with:

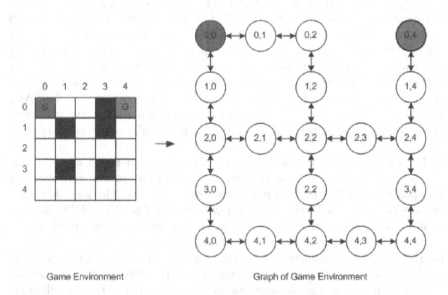

FIGURE 6.13   Implementation of an A* graph to find the best way.

open and closed lists. The empty list contains all the nodes that non-visited nodes, while the closed list contains all the visited nodes. The algorithm starts with a node available in the list and looks for nodes accessible from it, adding them to the empty list (if they are not already added in the closed list). Next, the current node's score is determined using the node's value (some of the nodes might be more expensive than others to pass through) and a heuristic from the current node (the shortest distance between a node and the goal). The process is carried out repeatedly until the desired result is obtained. Then, the algorithm follows the node's decreasing score back again to the starting node to determine the shortest path.

There are several path-finding algorithms, including A*. An original path-finding algorithm can cluster the universe into larger nodes in applications with a large set of maps and small-sized CPUs. On the other hand, hierarchical path-finding generated a smaller number of nodes, decreasing the amount of time spent looking.

6.3.3.3   Real-Time Play Complex AI

The growth of ML players in *Dota 2* is the final example we will look at. *Dota 2* is a real-time strategy game in which two teams of five players compete to demolish an ancient structure. Each of the team members works together to kill the ancients of the other while defending their own. This game features a variety of characters with varying playstyles (carry vs. support). Characters can increase their level to improve their ultimate skills and earn gold to buy products with unique properties. *Dota 2* has an interesting feature in that it takes a lot of coordination and collaboration to win.

In April 2019, OpenAI Five released an advanced *Dota 2* AI that beat the *Dota 2* e-sports world champions. With no previous knowledge of the game or heuristics to guide its behavior, the AI was designed from the ground up. It began by using a random weight initialization technique for its neural networks and then self-taught itself to play the game. In 80% of the games, the eligible AIs (5 for each character) competed against each other, and 20% against previous AIs. The AIs used 128,000 CPU cores and 256 GPUs to play 180 years' worth of games every day. Each game's AI makes about 20,000 moves, meaning a long time horizon for data collection to match an AI scenario. Thanks to a team spirit hyperparameter, OpenAI Five consists of five different neural networks that work together. As a result, individual AIs can focus on either their own reward (which involves killing other characters and gathering their treasure) or the team's overall reward (such as collecting treasure).

The three parts of AI are perception, processing, and action selection (see Figure 6.14). Different types of environmental inputs are fed into an embedding max-pooled as well as into the perception processing core. The long short-term memory (LSTM) is a Turing complete recurrent neural network (RNN) that can perform all of the computations of a general-purpose machine. Furthermore, LSTMs excel at learning sequences, making them ideal for this use. After that, the LSTM sends its production to a group of action networks, which decide what action to take (alongside the other pertinent information, like target). Furthermore, this takes into account the decisions that the character is free to take as well as the character's attention.

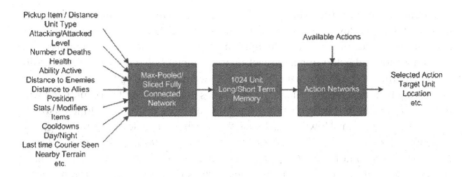

FIGURE 6.14 Dota 2 hero AI for long-horizon learning.

The agent's perception space is very large since the network's inputs are made up of around 20,000 real values. With about 170,000 total unique actions to choose from, the number of actions available is also very large (about 1,000 actions that are typically possible among them as they are reduced due to cooldowns, items not present, etc.). The OpenAI Five used proximal policy optimization for learning, which is simple to use and performs well in real-world scenarios. Both how we play games and how they are made are being transformed by AI. While the methods used have evolved over time, some ideas have remained unchanged, such as Arthur Samuel's principle of self-play in the creation of learning agents. From checkers and the IBM 701 to complex real-time games trained with the aid of distributed networks of CPUs and GPUs, ML is an integral part of games and a test-bed for potential ML methods [14].

6.4   CONCLUSION AND FUTURE SCOPE

AI is a powerful technology that can be used at any point of the game, from game design to customer loyalty and a realistic gaming experience. As a result, investing in ML solutions is important, as the advantages of AI in gaming cannot be overlooked. Furthermore, game developers can use all game development methods, track and evaluate player results, provide round-the-clock customer service, and improve their gaming experience with AI and its subset of understanding, ML. AI's advantages will continue to evolve and improve as games become more interactive, realistic, and lifelike. Intelligent actions in games will provide attractive features in virtual movement and interaction between game characters and game players. The game's protagonist can use sensors and actuators to interact with his surroundings and react appropriately. This character's action is edited by the coder, who then develops the character through observation and communication. Because of the existence and incorporation of IoT and AI, all of this is possible. AI is paving the way for a future centered on custom-made games.

Learning is the next big thing in game AI. Instead of making all NPC actions predetermined when a game is published, it should evolve, learn, and adapt as it is played. As a result, as the player progresses, the game becomes more difficult to foresee, extending the game's lifespan. Since learning and changing games are inherently unpredictable, AI developers have historically approached learning strategies with caution. Non-deterministic AI, which has its own set of problems, encompasses the techniques for understanding and reacting to character behavior. However, building and evaluating non-deterministic learning AI techniques takes longer. In addition, debugging becomes more difficult as it becomes more difficult to comprehend what the AI is doing fully. These obstacles have proven to be major impediments to AI's widespread adoption. However, a lot of this is changing. Several famous games, including *Creatures, Black & White, Battlecruiser 3000AD, Dirt Track Racing, Fields of Battle,* and *Heavy Gear,* used non-deterministic AI. Their achievements sparked renewed interest in AI techniques such as decision trees, neural networks, genetic algorithms, and probabilistic methods. Non-deterministic methods are used in combination with more conventional deterministic methods in these success-ful games. They are used only when they are required and for problems for which they are ideally suited. A neural network is not a magic pill that will solve all AI problems in a game; however, it can be used with excellent results for specific AI tasks. When using non-deterministic methods, we suggest taking this approach. This way, you can isolate the parts of your AI system that are unpredictable and difficult to create, test, and debug while maintaining the majority of your AI system in its traditional form.

REFERENCES

1. Tamburrini, G. & Altiero, F. (2021). Research Programs Based on Machine Intelligence Games. In Chiodo, S. & Schiaffonati, V. (Eds.), Italian Philosophy of Technology. Philosophy of Engineering and Technology, vol 35. Springer, Cham. DOI: 10.1007/978-3-030-54522-2_11
2. Singh, T. & Mishra, J. (2021). Learning With Artificial Intelligence Systems: Application, Challenges, and Opportunities. In Verma, S. & Tomar, P. (Eds.), Impact of AI Technologies on Teaching, Learning, and Research in Higher Education (pp. 236–253). IGI Global, Hershey, Pennsylvania, 2021. DOI: 10.4018/978-1-7998-4763-2.ch015
3. Westera, W., Prada, R., Mascarenhas, S. et al. (2020). Artificial Intelligence Moving Serious Gaming: Presenting Reusable Game AI Components. Education and Information Technologies, 25, 351–380. DOI: 10.1007/s10639-019-09968-2
4. Ho, M. (2021, February 2). Video Games and Scientific Research. DOI: 10.31219/osf.io/cj593
5. Vamsidhar, E., Kanagachidambaresan, G.R., & Prakash, K.B. (2021) Application of Machine Learning and Deep Learning. In Prakash, K.B. & Kanagachidambaresan, G.R. (Eds.), Programming With TensorFlow. EAI/Springer Innovations in Communication and Computing. Springer, Cham. DOI: 10.1007/978-3-030-57077-4_8
6. Ahmad, F., Ahmed, Z., & Muneeb, S. (2021). Effect of Gaming Mode Upon the Players' Cognitive Performance During Brain Games Plays: An Exploratory Research. International Journal of Game-Based Learning, 11(1), 67–76. DOI: 10.4018/IJGBL.2021010105
7. Spronck, P., Liu, J., Schaul, T., & Togelius, J. (Eds.) (2020). Artificial and Computational Intelligence in Games: Revolutions in Computational Game AI: Report from Dagstuhl Seminar 19511. Schloss Dagstuhl-Leibniz-Zentrum fuer Informatik, Dagstuhl. https://drops.dagstuhl.de/opus/volltexte/2020/12011/

8. Yannakakis, G.N. & Togelius, J. (2015, December). A Panorama of Artificial and Computational Intelligence in Games. IEEE Transactions on Computational Intelligence and AI in Games, 7(4), 317–335. DOI: 10.1109/TCIAIG.2014.2339221

9. Yannakakis, G.N. & Togelius, J. (2018). Game AI Panorama. Artificial Intelligence and Games. Springer, Cham. DOI: 10.1007/978-3-319-63519-4_6

10. Yannakakis, G.N. & Togelius, J. (2018). Frontiers of Game AI Research. In Artificial Intelligence and Games. Springer, Cham. DOI: 10.1007/978-3-319-63519-4_7

11. Shao, K., Zhentao, T., Zhu, Y., Li, N., & Zhao, D. (2019). A Survey of Deep Reinforcement Learning in Video Games. DOI: https://arxiv.org/pdf/1912.10944.pdf

12. Bijl, J.L. & Boer, C.A. (2011). Advanced 3D Visualization for Simulation Using Game Technology. Proceedings of the 2011 Winter Simulation Conference (WSC), pp. 2810–2821. DOI: 10.1109/WSC.2011.6147985

13. Su, Y. (2018). The Application of 3D Technology in Video Games. Journal of Physics: Conference Series, 1087, 062024. DOI:10.1088/1742-6596/1087/6/062024

14. Khakpour, A., & Colomo-Palacios, R. (2020). Convergence of Gamification and Machine Learning: A Systematic Literature Review. Technology, Knowledge and Learning. DOI: 10.1007/s10758-020-09456-4

7 A Framework for Estimation of Generative Models Through an Adversarial Process for Production of Animated Gaming Characters

Saad Bin Khalid and Bramah Hazela

CONTENTS

7.1 Introduction 123
7.2 Literature Survey 125
    7.2.1 Unsupervised Representation Learning with Deep Convolutional Generative Adversarial Networks 126
    7.2.2 Conditional Generative Adversarial Networks 126
    7.2.3 Image Generation and Recognition 127
    7.2.4 Progressive Growing of GANs for Improved Quality, Stability, and Variation 129
    7.2.5 Diverse Image Generation via Self-Conditioned GANs 129
    7.2.6 Deformable GANs for Pose-Based Human Image Generation 130
    7.2.7 Systematic Analysis of Image Generation Using GANs 131
7.3 Methodology 131
    7.3.1 Working Intuition 132
    7.3.2 Architecture 132
    7.3.3 Training 133
7.4 Results 134
7.5 Conclusion 135
References 135

7.1 INTRODUCTION

Artificial intelligence has long been associated with gaming. Deep learning (DL) research has improved the consistency and innovations of games significantly. DL has proven to be a highly beneficial improvisation in game development. DL is used

DOI: 10.1201/9781003231530-7

to power various algorithms in gaming, including multiplayer, character control, voice recognition, avatar characteristics, and other areas. Generative Adversarial Networks (GANs), which Ian Goodfellow presented in 2014, have proven to be a significant improvement in the field of forgery (legally speaking) by automation. GANs are used in this chapter to create animated characters that can be used as avatars in games and generate various types of characters based on the data they were trained on.

It was decided to use Convolutional Neural Networks (CNNs) and transpose convolutions. The CGANs, or conditional GANs, are an update to the DCGANs, or deep convolutional GANs, which were an update to the standard GANs in the article. A Generator (a network of transpose convolutions for generating data from the vectors it receives) and a Discriminator are both used in GANs (a classification model that determines whether the images are authentic or generated by the Generator). Both of these networks are pitted against each other. The Generator's job is to convince the Discriminator that the fake images it produces are accurate. The Discriminator's job is to determine if the image is actual or generated by the Generator. Both Generator and Discriminator start dumb and are conditioned to become more competent at the same time when working against each other. We do not use any pre-trained models because an untrained model will struggle to compete with its much brighter counterpart. Adversary, resulting in the generation of pointless noise and, as a result, two useless models competing for no purpose [1].

DCGANs are an advancement over GANs in that they produce and distinguish between images using deeper networks. There are three significant steps in the training of both models in this phase. The all-convolutional net uses stride convolutions to replace deterministic spatial pooling functions like max-pooling, allowing the network to learn spatial down-sampling on its own. Both the Discriminator and the Generator have used the technique above, allowing the Generator to learn spatial up-sampling on its own. The second step is to remove the dense layers of convolutional features that are entirely connected on top. Global average pooling, which existing state-of-the-art image classification models use, is the best example that supports the method. Direct connections of the highest convolutional features to the Generator and Discriminator's input and output proved to be a good compromise. The GAN's first layer, which takes a uniform noise distribution as input, is completely connected since it is just matrix multiplication. However, the output is a reshaped four-dimensional (4D) tensor used as the convolution stack's first layer. The last convolutional layer in the Discriminator is flattened and fed into a single sigmoid output. The third step is Batch Normalization, which stabilizes learning by normalizing the input provided to each unit to achieve a zero mean and unit variance. This aids in resolving training issues that may occur as a result of poor initialization, and it also aids gradient flow in models with greater depth. This proved crucial for deep Generators to learn while avoiding the typical failure mode in GANs, where the Generator collapses all samples into a single stage. To prevent sample oscillation and model instability, batch normalization was not applied directly to the Generator's output layer and the Discriminator's input layer. Except for the Generator's output layer, which uses the Tanh function, the Generator uses the Leaky Rectified Linear Unit (ReLU) activation [2].

To train both models, CGANs are a better option. It works by giving both the networks, the Discriminator and the Generator, preconditioning and training them in a controlled manner. These make use of a separate Generator and Discriminator. If the Generator and Discriminator are initially preconditioned on some additional details, such as Y, the GANs can be upgraded to a conditional model. Y may be anything, like class codes, data from other modalities, or some other type of auxiliary data. If both networks are fed with Y as an extra layer of input, the conditioning can be done. The prior input noise and the information Y are combined in a joint hidden representation in the Generator. The adversarial training frame allows for considerable flexibility in how this hidden representation is composed. Y and the Generator's output are provided as inputs to a discriminative function in the Discriminator [3].

7.2 LITERATURE SURVEY

Ian Goodfellow proposes a novel framework for estimating generative models via an adversarial process in which two models are simultaneously trained: a generative model, the Generator, that receives the data distribution and builds an image using the received vectors, and a discriminative model, the Discriminator, that classifies whether a data sample belongs to the training data rather than having been produced by the Generator and estimates the probability of it being real or fake. The training technique for Generator is to maximize the classification error induced by the Discriminator. This structure is comparable to a two-player Minimax game. There is a particular solution in the space of arbitrary functions Generator and Discriminator, in which Generator recovers the Discriminator's training data distribution and updates the weights. When Discriminator and Generator are made up of multilayer perceptrons, backpropagation can train the entire machine for both Discriminator and Generator. Neither the training nor the generation of samples requires unrolled approximate inference networks or Markov chains [1].

The Generator is pitted against a rival in the proposed nets framework: a Discriminator, a network equipped to determine if the sample data obtained is from the Generator (or fake) or belongs to the actual data distribution. According to the person behind this model, the Generator can be thought of as a team of forgers attempting to counterfeit currency. In contrast, the Discriminator can be thought of as a team of detectives attempting to distinguish between fake and authentic currency. Both the forgers and the detectives improve their skills until they forged money that is almost indistinguishable from the real thing.

This model can be used to generate training algorithms for a variety of models and optimization algorithms. In this post, we will look at a unique situation. The Generator produces samples from random noise using a multilayer perceptron, while the Discriminator classifies the data as false or true using its multilayer perceptron. Both models can be trained on the dataset and samples from the Generator using commonly used and highly efficient backpropagation algorithms. There is no need for Markov chains or approximate inference.

7.2.1 UNSUPERVISED REPRESENTATION LEARNING WITH DEEP CONVOLUTIONAL GENERATIVE ADVERSARIAL NETWORKS

This research aims to close the gap between the effective use of CNNs for supervised and unsupervised learning. This chapter introduces DCGANs, which are superior to conventional GANs for image generation using CNNs. The architecture has been trained on various datasets, and the results show that the deep convolutional adversarial pair in both Discriminator and Generator has learned a hierarchy of representations. These newly acquired features are then used in more advanced tasks, such as demonstrating their utility in general image representation.

The authors' approach is based on adopting and modifying three recently demonstrated improvements to CNN architectures. First, the all-convolutional network replaces deterministic spatial pooling functions (like max-pooling) with stride convolutions, allowing the network to learn spatial down-sampling on its own. Both the Discriminator and the Generator have used the technique above, allowing the Generator to learn its spatial up-sampling.

On top of convolutional features, the removal of completely connected dense layers is the second step. Global average pooling, which existing state-of-the-art image classification models use, is the best example that supports the method. The direct relation of the highest convolutional features to the Generator and Discriminator's input and output proved a good compromise. The GAN's first layer, which takes a uniform noise distribution as input, is completely connected since it is just matrix multiplication. However, the output is a reshaped 4D tensor used as the convolution stack's first layer. The last convolutional layer in the Discriminator is flattened and feeds its data into a single sigmoid output.

Finally, Batch Normalization is a method of learning stabilization that involves normalizing the input provided to each unit to achieve a zero mean and unit variance. This aids in resolving training issues that may occur as a result of poor initialization, and it also aids gradient flow in models with greater depth. This proved crucial for deep Generators to learn while avoiding the typical failure mode in GANs, where the Generator collapses all samples into a single stage. To prevent sample oscillation and model instability, batch normalization was not applied directly to the Generator's output layer or the Discriminator's input layer. Except for the Generator's output layer, which uses the Tanh function, the Generator uses the Leaky ReLU activation.

The model's training progressed to the point that it saturated and filled the entire color space of the training data distribution. It was discovered that the Leaky rectified activation works well, particularly for higher resolution modeling. This was in contrast to the standard GAN's max-out activation previously used [2].

7.2.2 CONDITIONAL GENERATIVE ADVERSARIAL NETWORKS

In this chapter, we propose a conditional version of GANs, in which both the Generator and the Discriminator can be conditioned on data by simply feeding it into both networks. The model has been learned to generate Modified National Institute of Standards and Technology (MNIST) datasets, which contain binary images of handwritten digits based on class labels, according to the authors. The work also shows how the proposed model can be used to learn a multimodal model and gives examples of how it can be applied to image tagging, demonstrating how the method can generate descriptive tags that are not part of the training labels.

Using GANs to train generative models has proved to be a promising alternative. They are getting around the problem of approximating a large number of intractable probabilistic computations. Adversarial networks have the advantage of not requiring Markov chains or probabilistic intervention because gradients are obtained using backpropagation, and a wide range of incorporations and factors can be easily incorporated into the model. Furthermore, the networks will produce realistic samples and log-likelihood estimates that are up to date. The modes of data generation are totally out of balance in a generative model that has not been conditioned. However, using some additional information to condition the model, the data generation process can be guided. For inpainting, the conditioning could use data from a particular modality, class marks, or a portion of the data. This chapter is a demonstration of how to go about building CGANs. For analytical findings, two sets of experiments have been demonstrated. The model was trained on the MNIST digit dataset conditioned on class labels in one experiment and on the MIR Flickr 20.000 dataset for multimodal learning in the other.

The GANs can be upgraded to a conditional model if the two networks, the Generator and the Discriminator, are preconditioned on some additional details, say Y, before training. Y may be information from other modalities, class marks, or some other type of auxiliary data. As an extra layer of data, Y can be fed into both the Generator and the Discriminator to perform the conditioning. In the Generator, the obtained input noise and Y are combined in joint hidden representations. The adversarial training frame aids in imparting considerable versatility in how this hidden representation is implemented. Y and the output from Generator are provided as inputs to a discriminative function in the Discriminator [3].

7.2.3 IMAGE GENERATION AND RECOGNITION

This study takes a deep dive into recent GAN research, summarizing the various architectures and their implementations in various fields and methods for training GANs for optimal results and dealing with latent space. Following that, this chapter addresses possible future GAN research areas, including improving GAN assessment, exploring different techniques for GAN training, and gaining a deeper overall understanding of GANs. The report's second section examines the compiled picture dataset describing each of the seven fundamental human emotions and the experiments conducted when conditioning a StarGAN on this dataset and the FER2013 dataset [4].

This chapter talks about different GAN architectures that have been proposed since the idea of GANs was introduced in 2014 and discussed several techniques for training the GANs. This chapter talks about the following architectures:

i. **CGANs:** CGANs were introduced into the field to condition the GAN model and give it the ability to guide what it produces. This is accomplished by using the data as an additional input layer to condition both the Generator and the Discriminator models. One of the many benefits of CGAN is that it allows for better one-to-many mapping representation, which means that conditioning on a single class (e.g., cat) will synthesize a range of cats with different colors and features [3].

ii. **Stack GANs:** Stack GAN is a two-stage GAN that uses text descriptions to create photo-realistic images (proposed in 2016 by Zhang et al.). The problem is broken down into two simpler "stages," significantly improving on previous approaches. The first stage (Stage-I GAN) summarizes what is mentioned in the text before adding the primary context and object colors. The second stage (Stage-II GAN) takes both the text description and the low-resolution image generated in stage 1 as input. It performs image detailing to make it more photo-realistic and accurate to the text description [5].

iii. **Cyclical GANs:** Cyclical GANs function by using a cycle continuity loss, which allows information to be transferred from one domain to another and then back to the previous domain without loss. While cycle consistency loss had previously been used in other areas, the CycleGAN was the first time it was applied to GANs. The CycleGAN enables translation between two separate image domains by training on two unordered image sets, one for each domain. This is possible because the CycleGAN assumes an underlying relationship between the two domains, allowing for training without paired training data [4].

iv. **Self-attention GANs (SAGANs):** Long-range dependence modeling and self-attention are combined in the SAGAN to generate images of scenarios and artifacts linked in a way that is compatible with realistic images (proposed in 2018 by Zhang et al.). Self-attention looks for connections between different sections of a series in order to represent and recognize each one. The SAGAN is the first paradigm to incorporate self-awareness into GANs. In general, GAN models employ convolutional layers in their architecture since they are effective at modeling local dependencies, but CNN's fall short when it comes to long-range modeling dependencies. By applying self-attention to both networks, the SAGAN effectively models both local and global dependencies in an image, ensuring consistency in the highly detailed features in different portions of the created image [6].

The different training techniques this chapter discusses are:

i. **Feature matching:** Making the Generator's goal fit the expected value of the Discriminator's intermediate layers.

ii. **Minibatch discrimination:** Deals with mode collapse by making the Discriminator examine a small number of examples rather than a single example, allowing it to determine if the Generator is generating the same outputs. Feature matching was found to be inferior to this form.

iii. **Historical averaging:** By keeping track of the historical average, it penalizes significantly different criteria from the average.

iv. **One-sided label smoothing:** This approach lowers the Discriminator's goal to 0.9 from 1, preventing it from reaching overconfidence and, as a result, providing weak gradients.
v. **Virtual batch normalization:** Takes advantage of batch normalization, but instead of using it, it normalizes each sample using a reference batch set before the training begins. Since the Generator network is computationally intensive, this is only applied to it [4].

7.2.4 Progressive Growing of GANs for Improved Quality, Stability, and Variation

The study describes a new GAN training method. The strategy is to improve both the Discriminator and the Generator gradually. New layers are introduced as the training progresses, starting with a low-resolution image, modeling increasingly fine details. This stabilizes and speeds up the preparation, enabling us to produce images of unrivaled quality, such as CelebFaces Attribute (CELEBA) images at 1024². The research also proposes a simple method for increasing image variation and achieves an unsupervised CIFAR10 inception score of 8.80, a new high. The authors also go through some implementation specifics that are important to prevent unhealthy competition between Discriminator and Generator. Finally, the authors propose a metric for evaluating GAN performance based on the shaped image quality and variation in the images generated. Besides, the authors create a higher-resolution version of the CELEBA dataset [7].

However, this chapter's main contribution is a training method for GANs that requires starting with low-resolution images and gradually increasing the resolution by adding layers to the networks. Instead of trying to get into the finer details simultaneously, this increasingly finer image update helps the network learn the overall broader scope of the image delivery first and then turn its focus to more delicate tweaks that need to be done. A Discriminator and a Generator, which are opposites of each other and often evolve synchronously competing with each other, are used to learn and update their weights. Both layers in both networks are trainable during the training period. Any layers added to the networks are faded in gradually, preventing abrupt shocks to the layers that have already been trained for a lower resolution. As seen in the work, Progressive training has many advantages, such as the development of smaller images becoming more stable early on due to fewer modes and fewer class details. Compared to the final goal of discovering a mapping from latent vectors to 1024² pictures, increasing the resolution incrementally makes weight changes much more accessible. This method is conceptually similar to Chen and Koltun's work, which successfully stabilizes the training for sound megapixel image synthesis using WGAN-GP loss and LSGAN loss.

7.2.5 Diverse Image Generation via Self-Conditioned GANs

This chapter aims to introduce a simple but successful unsupervised technique for creating realistic and diverse photographs. Instead of training on manually annotated class labels, the model is trained and conditioned on labels derived automatically from clustering in the Discriminator's feature space. The approach's clustering phase automatically detects variable modes, which the Generator must specifically cover. Experiments on traditional mode collapse benchmarks show that the proposed technique outperforms most competing approaches to addressing mode collapse. Compared to previous approaches, the proposed methodology performs well on large-scale datasets like ImageNet and Places365, enhancing both standard quality metrics and image diversity.

The Generator collapses, generating minimal varieties of samples, resulting in the Generator's output distribution being much smaller than the support of actual data distribution. This is a crucial problem faced in generating a wide diversity of outputs in such a high-dimensional space as images. A class-CGAN, which specifically penalizes the Generator for not supporting each class, is one way to reduce mode collapse empirically. The authors propose to use this class-conditional architecture, but instead of accessing actual class labels, they synthesize labels in an unsupervised manner. The technique dynamically divides the real data space into several clusters at its most basic level, which are then used to train a class-CGAN. Since generation is conditioned on a cluster, index optimization is done about the corresponding conditioned Discriminator, with each Discriminator allocated to each cluster of the actual distribution. The proposed method enlivens the Generator's output data distribution, allowing it to cover any partition of the actual distribution. The data set is then partitioned into k clusters 1,..., k that are calculated during the training to train the GNN to synthesize the target distribution with perfect imitation following the actual distribution. There are no ground-truth labels used; instead, the samples are randomly clustered in the Discriminator feature space, and the clusters are modified regularly. A class-conditioned GAN architecture is used to separate the Generator and the Discriminator [8].

7.2.6 Deformable GANs for Pose-Based Human Image Generation

This chapter discusses the problem of generating a human image that resembles a specific pose that the image must be produced in. To be more specific, given an image of a person in a particular pose, an image of the same person in a different, alternative pose must be synthesized. The solution uses deformable skip connections in the network's Generator to deal with pixel-to-pixel misalignment caused by pose differences. Furthermore, a proposal for a nearest-neighbor loss is made in place of the usual L1 and L2 losses for matching the information of the rest of the created image with the target image. Compared to previous work in this field, the method used photographs of people in various poses, and the model outperforms the competition in two benchmarks. On the condition that the central point detector can extract the articulated object's pose, the proposed method can be used in the broader field of deformable object synthesis.

Local information can be transferred back and forth between the encoder and decoder parts of the Generator using the deformable skip connections. The local data that must be transferred is typically represented by a tensor, representing the feature map activations of the encoder's given convolutional layer. However, unlike before, the details to be shuttled must be chosen when taking into account object-shape deformation, as summarized by the discrepancy between P(xa) and P(xb) (xb). To do so, the global deformation is broken down into a series of local affine transformations, which are characterized by subsets of joints in P(xa) and P(xb) (xb). The content of F is deformed using these local masks and affine transformations built using the relevant joints, and then skip connections are used to copy the transformed tensor, which is then concatenated with the corresponding tensor in the destination layer [9].

7.2.7 SYSTEMATIC ANALYSIS OF IMAGE GENERATION USING GANS

In recent years, GNNs have played a critical role in the advancement and growth of unsupervised learning. The GANs, which are the epitome of image synthesis from text or other images, have outperformed conventional approaches in terms of efficiency. These Adversarial training networks aim to estimate the expected data distribution from the actual distribution and use that estimate as input in synthetic data generation. This basic concept can create a variety of frameworks that are eidolon implementations in various domains of real-life applications, such as high-resolution output generation, art synthesis, and image synthesis from human-drawn sketches, to name a few. Though GANs are an improvement over conventional approaches in principle, providing better outcomes in various areas, implementing these architectures for real-world critical applications remains a challenge. This research delves into and investigates these structures, including a glossary of terms and their applications in text-to-image and image-to-image synthesis. The GNNs are subjected to a series of crucial examinations, beginning with the basic architecture and progressing through the numerous changes and upgrades made to the frameworks. The advantages and disadvantages of using GNNs over other traditional methods have been examined and discussed and the industries' reliance on GNNs for betterment [8].

7.3 METHODOLOGY

a. **Convolutional layer:** For generating a feature map, this layer adds a feature detector, which is a 3×3 matrix of zeros and ones in general, to the image matrix, which is also binary. The feature detector strides through the image matrix, traversing it entirely, ANDed its inputs with the image matrix's inputs, performing the addition of the resulting matrix's components, and storing it in the feature map. After that, the resulting function map is a much smaller picture with missing data but highlighted essential features that can be used in a more streamlined manner later [10].

b. **Pooling layer:** This layer removes the important features even further and gives the neural network spatial variance so that the essential features can be skewed, turned, down, near, or lateral, and the model will still be able to classify them. In this case, a feature detector strides over the feature map from the convolutional layer without any feedback and generates a pooled feature map that is even smaller in scale. After that, the production is placed in the flattened sheet (a linear of features) [10].

c. **Kernel size:** The size of the kernel defines the field of view that comes under that convolution. A general choice for 2D is three—that is 3 × 3 pixels.

d. **Padding:** The padding specifies how a sample's border is treated. If the kernel is more significant than 1, a (half) padded convolution will hold the spatial output dimensions equal to the input. In contrast, unpadded convolutions will crop away some of the boundaries, reducing the output size. Padding aids in the management of production size.

e. **Stride:** The stride specifies the kernel's step size when traversing the image. The performance decreases as the stride lengthens. In the same way, that max-pooling uses a stride of 1, we can use a stride of 2 to down-sample a picture.

f. **Transpose convolution:** A transpose convolution is used to reconstruct the spatial resolution of the size of the output image and perform convolution resulting in a larger size image. It will be used in the construction of the Generator [10].

g. **Dense layer:** This is the fully connected layer that takes the inputs, assigns them with the wait, and is responsible for the activation caused by the features.

7.3.1 Working Intuition

GANs are trained using two models, a Discriminator and a Generator, that compete and work against each other while learning and updating their weights. The Generator's task is to produce images that resemble the images we are trying to generate to trick the Discriminator into thinking they are real-world images rather than created non-real images. The Discriminator's goal is to determine whether the images are natural or artificial. The Discriminator has been trained on both authentic and generated images (initially random noise). The parameters in both the Generator and the Discriminator are modified after each iteration. The Generator is given the parameters individually to correct its output rather than adding up the values and calculating the cost function as a whole [11].

Both the Generator and the Discriminator are trained at the same time to prevent one of the networks (the Discriminator) from being too bright for the other, resulting in random outputs because the Generator would not know which parameters to tweak to deceive the Discriminator.

7.3.2 Architecture

We start by creating a standalone Discriminator model with a 28 × 28 input image. A leakyReLU layer with an alpha of 0.2 is accompanied by a convolutional layer of 128 units with a scale of 3 × 3, a stride of 2, and padding of the same. This is accompanied by a leakyReLU layer with an alpha of 0.2 and a convolutional layer of 128 units with a scale of 3 × 3, a stride of 2, and padding as before. Finally, we flatten the layer and use the sigmoid function to complete the relation [11].

We also describe a standalone Generator that takes a 7 × 7 image as input and processes it through the dense layer before applying the leakyReLU layer with an alpha of 0.2. After that, a transpose convolution with a kernel size of 4 × 4 and a stride of 2 is used for up-sampling the 7 × 7 image from the previous layer to a 14 × 14 image. The 14 × 14 image obtained as input from the previous layer is then up-sampled to 28 × 28 using a transpose convolution with a kernel size of 4 × 4 and a stride of 2. Finally, the output is obtained using the Tanh layer [11].

After both the Discriminator and the Generator have been defined, we define the combined model comprising both the Generator and the Discriminator for updating the Generator. We make the Discriminator not trainable, get noise and input labels in the Generator and receive image outputs from it. Image output and label input from Generator are connected as inputs to Discriminator. GAN model is defined as taking in noise and label and outputting a classification. Finally, the model is compiled [12].

We first load the dataset, then pick authentic images, break the dataset into images and labels, and finally create class labels. Points in latent space must now be created as input for the Generator, which will then be used to construct fake examples with class labels.

Now that both the Generator and the Discriminator are ready, the next and final step is to train them together.

7.3.3 TRAINING

We first need to create two objects of the Discriminator class, one that receives the actual images. The Discriminator should learn to compute the high values, meaning the images are accurate for the Discriminator. Another that should learn to compute the low values, meaning the images are fake for the Discriminator. To accomplish this, we use the binary cross-entropy function [12].

The Generator tries to achieve the opposite goal to make the Generator assign high values to the fake images it creates.

Regularization is needed on both the Generator and the Discriminator, for which two different optimizers are created. It is critical to specify the variables these optimizers should change; otherwise, the Generator's optimizer might screw up the Discriminator's variables and vice versa.

Optimizers modify the weight parameters in order to minimize the loss function. The loss function serves as a reference to the terrain, indicating if the optimizer is heading in the right direction to meet the valley's bottom, the global minimum. The Adam optimizer is used in this situation.

The Adam optimizer follows this equation:

$$\theta_t + 1 = \theta_t - \frac{\alpha.\widehat{m_t}}{\sqrt{\hat{v}} + \mathcal{E}}$$

where,

$$\widehat{m_t} = \frac{m_t}{1-\beta_1^t}$$

$$\widehat{v_t} = \frac{v_t}{1-\beta_2^t}$$

$$m_t = (1-\beta_1)g_t + \beta_1 m_{t-1} \text{ and}$$

$$v_t = (1-\beta_2)g_t + \beta_2 v_{t-1}$$

where,
α is the step size,
β_1 and β_2 are decay rates,
m_t is the first-moment vector,
v_t is the second-moment vector, and
t in the subscript is the timestep.

Initially, the timestep is initialized as zero.

The first-moment vector and the second-moment vector are also initialized as zero for the timestep equal to zero.

β_1 has the value of 0.9, β_2 holds the value of 0.999, and as the timestep increases, both are raised to the powers of the timestep.

Adam algorithm first updates the exponential moving averages of the gradient (mt) and the squared gradient (vt), the first and second-moment estimates.

Hyper-parameters $\beta1$, $\beta2 \in [0, 1)$ control the exponential decay rates of these moving averages.

Moving averages are initialized as 0, leading to moment estimates biased around 0, especially during the initial timesteps. This initialization bias can be easily counteracted, resulting in bias-corrected estimates.

Finally, the parameters are updated.

Through balancing their losses, we also ensure that neither the Discriminator nor the Generator is too high. Otherwise, this would inhibit the learning of either part and could even obviate the network from learning anything at all. That is the reason that they trained at the same time.

The approach is to grow both Discriminator and the Generator progressively. Starting from a low resolution, new layers are added that model increasingly fine details as training progresses. This significantly stabilizes the training while also speeding it up, allowing use in producing images of much better quality [12].

7.4   RESULTS

The battle in GANs is not about having the Discriminator's highest accuracy and lowest loss. This would have the exact opposite result to what the model is aiming for. Instead, we want to train the Discriminator as much as possible to classify

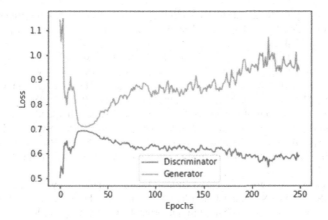

FIGURE 7.1 Graph of loss of Generator and Discriminator in CGAN.

accurate data (from the data distribution) and false data (Generator by the Generator), and then train the Generator to reduce the loss as much as possible. Both models are trained in parallel, with the idea that if one of them is too intelligent for the other, we will end up with two dumb models that cannot learn from each other.

The loss graph Generator in the training process has been shown in Figure 7.1.

The graph in Figure 7.1 has been attained after 100 epochs with a batch size of 32 images per batch. The model shows a decent performance in creating images since the graphics are not too demanding in the creation of animated images.

7.5 CONCLUSION

In terms of image creation, the model performs admirably. The Generator's batch normalization was not applied at first, resulting in a reduction in its efficiency. The learning significantly improved after batch normalization layers were applied. The dense layer had to be a balanced job in terms of size because a too large layer resulted in the model generating too similar images. Simultaneously, a too-small layer resulted in Generator failing to learn and update the weights effectively, resulting in distorted images. It must be ensured that the Generator does not overfit or underfit, and tuning must be meticulous.

REFERENCES

1. Generative Adversarial Nets by Ian J. Goodfellow, Jean Pouget-Abadie, Mehdi Mirza, Bing Xu, David Warde-Farley, Sherjil Ozair, Aaron Courville, Yoshua Bengi. https://arxiv.org/pdf/1406.2661.pdf
2. Unsupervised Representation Learning With Deep Convolutional Generative Adversarial Networks. Alec Radford & Luke Metz, Soumith Chintala. https://arxiv.org/pdf/1511.06434v2.pdf
3. Conditional Generative Adversarial Nets by Mehdi Mirza, Simon Osindero. https://arxiv.org/pdf/1411.1784.pdf

4. CSGAN: Cyclic-Synthesized Generative Adversarial Networks for Image-to-Image Transformation by Kishan Babu Kancharagunta, Shiv Ram Dubey. https://arxiv.org/abs/1901.03554

5. A Style-Based Generator Architecture for Generative Adversarial Networks by Tero Karras, Samuli Laine, Timo Aila. https://arxiv.org/abs/1812.04948v3

6. Self-Attention Generative Adversarial Networks by Han Zhang, Ian Goodfellow, Dimitris Metaxas, Augustus Odena. https://arxiv.org/abs/1805.08318v2

7. Progressive Growing of GANS for Improved Quality, Stability, and Variation by Tero Karras, Timo Aila, Samuli Laine, Jaakko Lehtinen. https://arxiv.org/pdf/1710.10196.pdf

8. Systematic Analysis of Image Generation using GANs by Rohan Akut, Sumukh Marathe, Rucha Apte, Ishan Joshi, Siddhivinayak Kulkarni. https://arxiv.org/abs/1908.11863

9. Deformable GANs for Pose-based Human Image Generation by Aliaksandr Siarohin, Enver Sangineto, Stephane Lathuili, and Nicu Sebe. https://openaccess.thecvf.com/content_cvpr_2018/papers/Siarohin_Deformable_GANs_for_CVPR_2018_paper.pdf

10. Convolutions: Transposed and Deconvolution. https://medium.com/@marsxiang/convolutions-transposed-and-deconvolution-6430c358a5b6

11. Conditional and Controllable Generative Adversarial Networks. https://towardsdatascience.com/conditional-and-controllable-generative-adversarial-networks-a149691ddae6

12. Implementing a Generative Adversarial Network (GAN/DCGAN) to Draw Human Faces. https://towardsdatascience.com/implementing-a-generative-adversarial-network-gan-dcgan-to-draw-human-faces-8291616904a

8 Generative Adversarial Networks Based PCG for Games
A Comprehensive Study

Nimisha Mittal, Priyanjali Pratap Singh, and Prerna Sharma

CONTENTS

8.1 Introduction 138
8.2 Background 140
    8.2.1 Procedural Content Generation (PCG) 140
        8.2.1.1 Game Bits 140
        8.2.1.2 Game Space 140
        8.2.1.3 Game Systems 140
        8.2.1.4 Game Scenarios 141
        8.2.1.5 Game Design 141
        8.2.1.6 Derived Content 141
    8.2.2 Procedural Content Generation Using Machine Learning
        (PCGML) 141
    8.2.3 Deep Learning in PCG 142
    8.2.4 Generative Adversarial Networks 142
8.3 Overview of GAN in Video Games 142
    8.3.1 Level/Map Generation 143
    8.3.2 Height Map Generation 144
    8.3.3 Texture Synthesis in Games 145
    8.3.4 Characters or Face Generation 145
8.4 Overview of Datasets and Games 146
    8.4.1 Popular Games 146
        8.4.1.1 Super Mario Bros (1985) 146
        8.4.1.2 The Legend of Zelda (1986) 148
        8.4.1.3 DOOM (1993) 148
        8.4.1.4 Pac-man (1980) 148
        8.4.1.5 StarCraft (1998) 149
    8.4.2 Popular Datasets 149
        8.4.2.1 Video Game Level Corpus (VGLC) 149
        8.4.2.2 Idgames Archive 149

DOI: 10.1201/9781003231530-8

          8.4.2.3   General Video Game AI (GVG-AI) 150
          8.4.2.4   Sarah and Lucy Character 150
          8.4.2.5   NASA SRTM30.. 150
8.5   Future Advancement.. 151
8.6   Conclusion 152
References... 153

8.1   INTRODUCTION

Procedural Content Generation (PCG) is the automation of content production through algorithmic means. The content can be anything that requires the involvement of humans, from the creation of images to videos, poetry to music, paintings to architectural designs. Owing to its capability to augment human creativity, with limited or no human contribution, PCG has been an integral aspect of game development and technical games research for years now. The increasing prominence of PCG in games is due to its promising potential to escalate the replay values, reduce development costs and effort, optimize storage space, or simply improvise the aesthetics. With games as the prime focus, PCG refers to the creation of game contents, such as textures, maps, levels, quests, characters, stories, ecosystems, sound effects, weapons, or even game mechanics, player interaction, and rules.

PCG for games is broadly divided into two categories, namely functional and cosmetic. The functional PCG covers aspects like game space, systems, and scenarios [1], which includes maps, ecosystems, levels, and stories, etc. This majorly focuses upon the player interaction and game mechanics to enable state-of-the-art game experiences and enable adaptivity in games as per the player. The cosmetic PCG, on the other hand, focuses upon graphics and visualization, vegetation, architecture, textures, and sounds. It also includes the set of rules and mechanics of the game that constitute the game design [1].

The most sought-after and elusive goals of PCGs are to achieve the ability to control the generated content (controllability), express a variety of unrepetitive content (expressivity), and generate believable content (believability) [2]. The techniques used in applications of PCG in games to achieve these goals are broadly categorized as constructive or traditional and artificial intelligence-based (AI-based). The simpler traditional approaches have been to use grammars, noise-based algorithms, fractals, Pseudo-random number Generators. The AI-based techniques are further classified into search-based, solver-based, machine learning-based (ML-based), and subsequently, deep learning-based (DL-based). The search-based methods [3] employed evolutionary algorithms and stochastic and metaheuristic search/optimization techniques, while solver-based methods [4] use the design space approach to function. The need to be fine-tuned or even explicitly be designed for specific generations is the primary flaw in standard/constructive PCG that gave rise to the development and advancement of ML-based PCG (MLPCG). MLPCG aims to design general algorithms that can create vast amounts of content using reasonable amounts of data. ML-based methods have a wide category of algorithms to choose from, such as n-grams, Markov models, Recurrent neural networks, autoencoders to name a few. Some of the most famous algorithms deployed under DL methods are neural networks, Generative adversarial networks (GANs) [5], deep variational autoencoders (VAEs) [6], and long short-term memory (LSTM) [7, 8]. The dependency of most algorithms on initial designs from humans for future automatic developments opens up the gateway for research on DL-based game mechanics, capable of crafting algorithms, parameters, constraints, and objectives for games without human intervention.

The method under consideration in this chapter is GANs, a two-deep neural networks-based ML algorithm. The most common issues observed in Procedural Content Generation using machine learning (PCGML) are ill-detailed content generation, unguaranteed playability, unavailability of training data, and poor creation of personalized content [9]. The two networks in GANs, a Discriminator and Generator, that work in tandem and in opposition to develop content, show the potential to produce high-quality content as well as appropriate identification of unplayable games—two of the most grieve problems. Being statistically and computationally efficient, GANs have emerged as one of the most successful frameworks that are based on unsupervised generative modeling [10]. Depending upon the dataset on which the model is trained, the content can be partial or complete, autonomous, interactive, or guided [9], stochastic or deterministic, necessary or optional [2].

Following the boom in the field of AI, there has been considerable exploration of AI implementation in games. As opposed to highly recognized Atari 2600 games that were used as the benchmark for visual learning algorithms [11], attention has shifted toward AI-backed games to provide a more realistic gaming experience. First-person shooting games have been the first choice to test new algorithms by a fairly large number of researchers for their ease of utilization and examination. There have been steady-state genetic algorithms [12], rule base evolution-based algorithms such as REALM [13], Hybrid Fuzzy ANN Systems [14], navigation by imitation via Playback of human movement [15] among many others. The convolutional deep neural network-based VizDoom [11], a highly customizable lightweight and fast software that is based on the classical first-person shooter (FPS) video game, Doom, garnered attention from the industry for its rudimentary approach to visual reinforcement learning in three-dimensional (3D). Perhaps the most popular milestone in this endeavor are the uses of Deep Convolutional Generative Adversarial Network (DCGAN) [16], Token-based One-shot Arbitrary Dimension GANs (TOAD-GANs) [17], and LSTMs [18] in the game Mario to evolve levels. Furthermore, to create photorealistic co-creative level designs, VAEs [19] generate level segments that can combine properties of levels from two different games—Kid Icarus and Super Mario. The antagonistic nature of the two neural nets used in GANs presents significant similarity with games and hence it has been the area of interest to many developers. A noteworthy development is the creation of GameGAN [20], a regenerative deterministic and stochastic modeling algorithm. The most successful implementation of GameGAN has been on Pac-Man, where visual imitation of the desired game is learned by the model to create newer aspects for the game, by enhancing the interpretability and providing high visual consistency.

The review of the application of GANs in the field of gameplay content generation is divided into two parts. Initially, the research based on PCG is explored to gain a broad yet well-elucidated understanding of PCG and its classification. This is followed by shifting the focus on GAN and in particular to their application in games PCG and a compendious overview of games based on GANs to study their compelling nature.

Following the introduction, this chapter is further segregated into different sections that include: Section 8.2, which gives a brief overview of earlier research done in the field of PCG, and Section 8.3 presents our review regarding these algorithms. Section 8.4 describes the various games along with datasets utilized in them. Section 8.5 provides a brief overview of potential future direction of research for GANs in video games. Finally, Section 8.6 includes the conclusion.

8.2 BACKGROUND

Further, this section presents reviews of PCG along with its implementation via ML and DL methodologies for several video games. Further, the procedural generation of game contents (six classes) using different approaches is analyzed.

The comprehensive exploration of these algorithms highlighted the recent exploration of GAN and its implementation by several scholars. However, the literature available is extremely limited and has not been structured properly for future research in the same domain.

8.2.1 PROCEDURAL CONTENT GENERATION (PCG)

With the propitious stature of PCG, it is natural for it to be able to create countless aspects of games and therefore it is of the obvious need to classify the aspects into recognizable categories. Following are the six categories [1, 2] under which the procedurally generated content can be classified into.

8.2.1.1 Game Bits

Game bits are considered the primary elements of any game content that can be either essential or unimportant for the game. This categorization depends on whether the game bits are concrete or abstract. However, it is notable that these components independently cannot be sufficient for user interactions. Vegetation and buildings are examples of the concrete domain that could be interacted directly within the game environment while other abstract units such as texture and background music need to be combined with other components for creating a concrete unit.

8.2.1.2 Game Space

Game space is referred to as the surrounding environment of the game that a player interacts with where several game bits. Similar to game bits, game spaces can also be categorized as either concrete or abstract. Game space is considered the most crucial part of a game as it is responsible for making the gameplay interesting for the players. Indoor maps, outdoor maps, and bodies of water are the three main types of this game content.

8.2.1.3 Game Systems

It generates and simulates complex surrounding in the game that makes the gameplay more realistic and appealing for the players. These systems include urban environment, road network, and ecosystems along with complex player interaction with the virtual world that makes these games more real-life.

8.2.1.4   Game Scenarios

The sequence in which the events of the game will be used to make player interaction is depicted by game scenarios. These consistently keep the users engrossed in the games by challenging the players with different types of problems to accomplish. Puzzles, stories, storyboards are some of the common types of scenarios that are generally present in any game. Additionally, the concept of level has always been a key element in the creation of games that keeps players motivated to reach their goals.

8.2.1.5   Game Design

Game designs are another important element of gameplay that is in charge of maintaining a balance between all the players. Specifically, these designs generate several game rules to be followed while playing and the goals that have to be achieved by the players.

8.2.1.6   Derived Content

This module makes players be more immersed in the gameplay by providing them with tools to access and review their experiences in-game. News or broadcasts and leaderboards are two main examples of these types of content that are used in almost every arcade game.

8.2.2   Procedural Content Generation Using Machine Learning (PCGML)

PCGML [9] concepts is based on creating novel content for arcades by initially training the model of existing content of the gameplay available. ML has been used for several applications when integrated with PCG such as in autonomous content generation, creating co-creative and mixed-initiative design where AI assists humans for gameplay content creation. PCGML due to its approach to use training on existing data has been able to identify repair areas (not playable) and analyze the generated components. Moreover, initially, PCG was introduced to compress game data due to a lack of disk space.

There are several areas in game content where PCGML has been applied, like real-time-based strategy levels, collectible card generation in arcade games, and integration of interactive fiction. However, it has been evident from the research in this domain that the major focus has always been on level generation problems. For instance, the n-grams method was used by Dahlskog et al. [21] on original Super Mario Bros. gameplay to create new levels. Further, this domain and Super Mario data were explored by Jain et al. [22] by applying the concept of autoencoders. Snodgrass and Ontan integrated Multi-Dimensional Markov chains with PCG[23]. They have surveyed Markov chains in-depth to ensure usable and higher levels for gameplay. Furthermore, Bayes Net and Principal Component Analysis (PCA) [24] have been implemented on *Legend of Zelda* for level and room creation. Researchers have also worked on predicting resource locations on StarCraft II maps using neural networks [25].

8.2.3 Deep Learning in PCG

Recently, DL is having a great impact in the field of PCG [26] by integrating several techniques including GAN [5], reinforcement learning such as LSTM [7, 8], VAEs [6], and evolutionary computing. These methods have generally been employed to generate creative game content, however, sometimes these generated results require certain adaptations for creating content that is practical to use. Of these, reinforcement learning is a recent domain being explored in the field of arcades. Similar to PCGML, most researches in DLPCG to date focus majorly on generating playable levels [26]. Another interesting area in DLPCG is the implementation of GAN in gameplay content generation that will be discussed in detail in Section 8.3.

8.2.4 Generative Adversarial Networks

GANs [5] are one of the most prominent deep generative models that are based on adversarial training techniques. It can be assumed to be an adversarial game between two players, Generator (G) and Discriminator (D) whose objective is to maintain the Nash Equilibrium (NE). Hence, the basic principle behind adversarial networks is to map a random noise vector through a Generator to generate a sample. This resultant is further analyzed by the Discriminator to classify the sample as real or fake. Training these adversaries ensures the Discriminator achieves a maximum state of correctly distinguishing the generated samples.

At present, GANs are being extensively employed in different fields such as computer vision and natural language processing for several tasks. In vision-related systems, GANs are being applied for image translation, improving the resolution of images, texture synthesis, face synthesis, and image colorization. While in the domain of natural language processing (NLP), music generation, and dialogue generation. Moreover, GANs have also been applied to the medical domain for solving different problems. Furthermore, adversarial learning is being employed in the area of video games for various generation tasks that will be elaborated in the next section.

8.3 OVERVIEW OF GAN IN VIDEO GAMES

This section gives a brief overview regarding different approaches been employed in gameplay content generation using the concept of adversarial learning. GANs and their variants are the most popular model being explored recently for several tasks. In the area of games, to date, they have been mostly used for either 2D or 3D level/ map generation, along with certain research in creating face/characters for game and texture synthesis for game modules. Figure 8.1 represents the rate of evolution of GAN in the area of arcade games. We will discuss all the research in this field in detail in subsequent subsections.

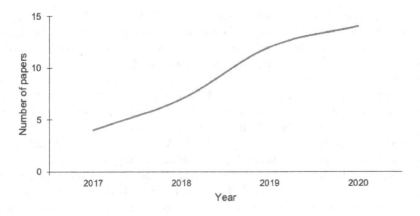

FIGURE 8.1   Evolution of GAN in video games.

8.3.1   Level/Map Generation

Level generation is the process that is responsible for creating a playable and interesting environment or scenarios for gameplay and is the most important aspect of any video game. Fabricating levels require designers to have both artistic and technical acumen. Generating the arcade maps requires extensive playtesting, hence, from the past few years, designers have inclined toward exploiting the domain of ML for modeling-level designs. Video games are either generate 2D levels or convert these to 3D maps for creating advanced games. There has been the implementation of several techniques to create levels using PCG. However, recently GANs [5] have emerged to be the most popular deep generative method for arcade content generation.

In 2018, Giacomello et al. [27] applies the concept of GAN for generating new and unique levels on *DOOM* [28] video game series. Their approach included implementing Wasserstein GAN with Gradient Penalty (WGAN-GP) in two ways. The first one only had images and noise vector as the input to the model and was named as unconditional WGAN-GP. On the other hand, in conditional WGAN-GP there is an additional input of extracted features from existing DOOM levels that showed better results in comparison to the unconditional model. Volz et al. [16] processed another popular game by Nintendo, Super Mario Bros [29] for stage creations. In this research, the main intent was to generalize the generation process for different games, hence, the authors divided the technique into two phases. In the first stage, an unsupervised method is used to train the GAN model which is followed by identifying ideal input vectors from the latent space. However, to avoid random sample generation evolutionary control in the form of Covariance Matrix Adaptation Evolution Strategy (CMA-ES) [30] is applied while exploring the inputs followed by fitness function evaluation. This procedure is extended by Giacomello et al. [31] where they used the CMA-ES technique on DOOM to generate novel levels according to the features required in the new gameplay stage. Prominently three types of levels were considered for this experiment, arena level, labyrinth level, and complex level.

The education domain is considered challenging for creating video games by applying PCG due to its requirement of fulfilling the learning objectives through it.

Therefore, there has been limited research in this field. However, Park et al. [32] proposed a multistep DCGAN (deep convolutional GAN) for generating novel and solvable levels. The model comprises two Generators, where the first one is responsible for creating a large dataset of synthetic levels from a small set of example stages. The generated data is further fed to the second Generator to produce levels with increased solvability. Furthermore, Torrado et al. [33] proposed conditional embedding self-attention generative adversarial network (CESAGAN) where the bootstrapping technique was integrated to efficiently train Generators and Discriminators. The model is based on combining self-attention GAN (SAGAN) [34] with a conditional vector to improve the diversity, uniqueness, and playability of the generated levels.

Gutierrez and Schrum [35] integrated both GAN and graph grammar to generate dungeon rooms for *The Legend of Zelda* [36] video game. In their initiated work, the model employs both GAN and graph grammar equally that resulted in the generation of an interesting and playable dungeon layout with the placement of obstacles and items in it. Followed by this research, Schrum et al. [37] combined GAN and Compositional Pattern Producing Network (CPPN) [38] to tackle the issue of arranging structured levels using segments. The CPPN exploited the latent vectors that are directly associated with game segments that resulted in the generation of complete levels.

Furthermore, Awiszus et al. [17] introduced TOAD-GAN, a unique methodology to generate new Mario levels by considering the scarcity of data. The proposed technique is based on SinGAN architecture [39] and employs a single training level to produce tile-based game stages. Bontrager and Togelius [40] have recently proposed a notable methodology on a 2D dungeon crawling game by implementing Generative Playing Networks (GPN). The model comprises of Generator and agent that have direct communication for generation of gameplay levels that results in the requirement of less training data. Moreover, Constrained Adversarial Networks (CANs) by Di Liello et al. [41] penalizes the GAN network for inappropriate and invalid structure generation. The application of CAN has produced efficient results without affecting the run-time of the model. Moreover, GameGAN, the recent development by NVIDIA [20] has integrated deterministic and modeling algorithms on Pac-Man to generate novel aspects related to the gameplay and providing high visual consistency.

Apart from specific models, there have been research on developing a general method for game content generation. The first one is introduced by Irfan et al. [42] where the model consists of DCGAN being train on three different games including Colourescape, Zelda, and Freeway. It was observed through this research that the generated stages were playable and a large amount of data assisted DCGAN to capture required data in the levels. Another approach was initiated by Kumaran et al. [43], in this approach branched GAN was trained that can generate levels of four different arcades using a single random vector as the input to the architecture and captures the variation present in the data while training.

8.3.2 HEIGHT MAP GENERATION

In computer graphics, height maps are the 2D projected image of points for displacing the 2D mesh to create the 3D terrain. Creating interactive 3D landscapes is essential for user interactions and to maintain the engagement of players. Moreover, as modeling of level maps might require a height map, researchers have also explored the domain of generating height maps from 2D images. As compared to the domain of level generation, research resources are limited in the area of height map generation. Broadly there have been four works on producing height maps in video games using GANS.

Beckham and Pal [44] in their research identified the first technique to generate height and texture maps using GANs. Initially, they trained their data on DCGAN to produce height maps that were further processed using pix2pix GAN for generating their corresponding textures. As shown in that research, they rendered height and texture maps to generate 3D terrain for video games. Furthermore, Wulff-Jensen et al. [45] in 2018 worked on Digital Elevation Maps (DEM) for alps [46] to generate 3D landscapes for enhancing gameplay interactivity. They trained DCGAN on Elevation Maps and then converted the same to 3D maps with Unity3D. The resultant maps were realistic and could be deployed while creating different arcade games.

In 2019, Spick and Walker [47] worked on creating a model that could generate several variants of a specific landscape region. For this purpose, they trained Spatial GAN (SPA-GAN) [48] with non-spatial feature learning. The height and texture maps were rendered through a 3D game engine to produce realistic and endless variants of any specific area.

Recently, there has been a novel approach to generate terrain for gameplays using rough sketches. Wang and Kurabayashi [49] proposed a unique methodology involving a generative model of two phases where the conditional generative adversarial network (cGAN) is responsible for generating different variants of elevation bitmap of the sketch. The model in this phase generates maps corresponding to the terrain data that has been used for training. In the second phase, the deterministic algorithm produces the actual asset for the terrain by interpreting the details on the elevation bitmap. Hence, this approach will help various designers to create interactive game maps by simply converting their rough sketches.

8.3.3   Texture Synthesis in Games

Texture synthesis is an essential component for enhancing realism in game content and makes the environment more aesthetic for game players. This enhancement eventually increases the interactivity of the arcade with the users. Moreover, it is evident from earlier research work that texturing is either applied through supervised or automated methods. However, the research in the field of synthesizing textures for gameplay content is a limited single experiment by integrating it with GANs.

Fadaeddini et al. [50], in their research, proposed a novel technique to apply texture synthesis for PCG in video games. They constructed a simple adversarial network where the network is trained on sample images of textures collected and then generated game levels using those textures.

8.3.4   Characters or Face Generation

Sprites are 2D animations or bitmap images that are integrated into the video game. These gameplay elements are not static and perform animation by moving independently. In games, they represent the users in the gameplay by acting as an interface between game players and the game environment. There have been several studies on generating sprites through PCG. Nevertheless, in this subsection, we will discuss their generation with the help of GANs.

Horsley and Perez-Liebana [51] introduced the technique of integrating DCGAN to generate sprites in video games. They considered three categories for analysis including Faces, Creatures, and Human-like sprite generation. Each of these categories produced satisfactory results even with a small dataset, however, at certain points the model needs to have a higher epoch count for better results.

Another interesting research by Hong et al. [52] proposes Multi-Discriminator GAN (MDGAN) that the unique sprites could be generated by only considering three image-related parameters; color, shape, and animation involved. The approach involves encoder networks for shape and color extraction while the decoder processes each encoder's inputs and applies a Discriminator network for these sprites. This methodology performs image-to-image translation for the 2D production of sprites.

In 2019, Serpa and Rodrigues [53] performed research on generating enhanced gameplay sprites using GANs. Hence, they designed a variant of the pix2pix model that comprises two parts. In the first part, there is a line-to-gray algorithm that converts the initial sprite lines to grayscale which is followed by conversion to colored sprites using a gray-to-color algorithm. The results obtained from this model depict enhancement in the quality of sprites as they involve the shading effect.

Table 8.1 depicts the main contributions of each GAN in each subdomain of gameplay content generation along with their short description.

8.4 OVERVIEW OF DATASETS AND GAMES

This section gives a brief elucidation on different games that are being used for the intent of research in the domain of PCG using GAN following their corresponding datasets from which they are extracted.

8.4.1 POPULAR GAMES

Games have always been favored by people from all generations and hence this area has innately advanced with time. Earlier the games used to be created manually, after which methods for automatic creation were examined, leading the interest toward PCG algorithms for the same. However, in recent years researchers are becoming interested in integrating them with advanced techniques like GANs for richer and enhanced content. However, throughout this period, certain games have been admired by researchers for experiments. Therefore, in this subsection, we will discuss some of those favorable games.

8.4.1.1 Super Mario Bros (1985)

Super Mario Bros [29] is a classical side-scrolling platform game, developed by Nintendo. With different power-up options, the evaluation for the games starts with Mario in a normal state, only capable of left-right scrolling and jumping. The game

TABLE 8.1
Main Contributions of the Above Explored Algorithms

Game Content Type	Variant	Author	Short Description
Map/Level Generation	WGAN-GP for DOOM Levels [7]	Giacomello et al.	Implemented WGAN with gradient penalty in conditional and unconditional way
	Mario Levels with DCGAN [33]	Volz et al.	Integrated the concept of latent space and CMA-ES to generate Mario Levels
	WGAN-GP with Latent Space [34]	Giacomello et al.	Extended WGAN-GP by employing latent space search
	Multistep DCGAN [35]	Park et al.	Developed educational game based on DCGAN
	CESAGAN [36]	Torrado et al.	Based on SAGAN and bootstrapping technique for improved performance
	GAN Rooms for Zelda [37]	Gutierrez and Schrum	Incorporated GAN and graph grammar to generate rooms
	CPPN2GAN [38]	Schrum et al.	Utilized CPPN to generate complete levels with segments
	TOAD-GAN [17]	Awiszus et al.	Based on implementation of SinGAN and single level training data on Mario dataset
	Generative Paying Networks [40]	Bontrager and Togelius	Architecture similar to GAN with Discriminator replaced to agent for direct communication
	Constrained Adversarial Network [41]	Di Liello et al.	Novel method where GAN penalizes network for invalid generated content
	Game Gan [20]	Kim et al.	Integrated deterministic and modelling algorithms on Pac-Man
	DCGAN based General PCG [42]	Irfan et al.	Generated playable levels by training the GAN architecture on 3 datasets
	Branched GAN based General PCG [43]	Kumaran et al.	Based on concept on random vector and variation training
Height Map Generation	Terrain Generation using DCGAN [44]	Beckham and Pal	Generation of 3d height maps using DCGAN and pix2pix GAN
	Height Map using DEM [45]	Wulff-Jensen et al.	Enhanced gameplay interactivity using digital elevation maps of alps
	Height and Texture Map using SPA-GAN [47]	Spick and Walker	Trained Spatial-GAN on non-spatial features to produce endless variants
	Sketch2Map [49]	Wang and Kurabayashi	Utilized conditional GAN and deterministic algorithm
Texture Synthesis	Texture Synthesis in Video Games [50]	Fadaeddini et al.	Applied texture synthesis of custom created dataset on game images
Character or Face Generation (Sprites)	Sprite Generator with DCGAN [51]	Horsley and Perez-Liebana	Integrated DCGAN for three categories, human-characters, faces and creatures
	Game Sprite using MDGAN [52]	Hong et al.	Implemented multi-Discriminator GAN and image-to-image translation
	Pixel Art for games [53]	Serpa and Rodrigues	Employed variant of pix2pix with line-to-gray and gray-to-color algorithm

consists of eight "worlds," each world with its own set of four sub-levels called "stages."

Each game starts with players having a certain number of lives and which may be increased by gaining additional lives by defeating several enemies in a row with a Koopa shell, picking up certain power-ups, or by collecting a certain number of coins or bouncing on enemies successively without getting in contact with the ground. Contact with enemies converts him into big mode and subsequent contact with enemies converts him into the regular state, instead of dying. The lives count decreases if Mario takes damage while small, falls in a bottomless pit, or exceeds the time limit. Once the lives count strikes zero, Mario dies and the evaluation ends.

8.4.1.2   The Legend of Zelda (1986)

The Legend of Zelda [36] is an action-adventure dungeon crawler, from Nintendo. The major genres explored in the game are puzzles, action, adventure/battle gameplay, and exploration itself. The three principal areas in the games are overworld, interconnection of all the areas; areas of interaction with other characters; and dungeons, the areas of labyrinthine layout wherein most of the gameplay occurs. The main character, Link, explores the overworld to find and explore several maze-like dungeons full of enemies, traps, and puzzles and takes aid to complete his missions by gaining special items or advice from other characters, or purchase equipment, or even complete side quests in the interaction areas.

The evaluation progresses as the player completes the assigned tasks without depleting the life meter. The life meter drops with combats with dungeon bosses and can be increased beyond just three hearts by attaining "Heart Containers." At the start of the evaluation, the player is given the extendable string of three hearts, representing the number of hits that can be withstood before the end of the evaluation.

8.4.1.3   DOOM (1993)

Developed by id Software, *Doom* [28] is a classical early 3D graphics-based FPS game, for MS-DOS. The game has a series of levels, with increasing difficulties, and several distinct levels constitute episodes. The game features three episodes: "Knee-Deep in the Dead," "The Shores of Hell," and "Inferno." The continuous succession in completion of levels in an episode progresses to entry in the next episode.

Evaluation requires exploration of some military base, in each level, in search of exits by the player as the protagonist character, Doomguy. While traversing the base, the player is required to defeat enemies in each level while managing supplies of ammunition, health status, and armor points. With each combat, the health points, armor points, and ammunition of the player decreases owing to the damage incurred during the combat. The player can replenish the depleted points by collecting power-ups, weapons, and ammunition throughout the levels and from defeated enemies. The evaluation ends as and when the health points cease to zero.

8.4.1.4   Pac-man (1980)

Developed by Namco, *Pac-Man* [54] is a maze chase arcade video game. The gameplay requires controlling an eponymous character, Pac-man, through an enclosed maze, populated with four varieties of enemies, that are presented as ghosts-Inky (cyan), Clyde (orange), Pinky (pink), and Blinky (red). Each ghost is given its own unique and distinct "personality," and operates differently, albeit with the same goal to catch the protagonist. The aim is to eat all the dots are in the maze, consistently avoiding the ghosts. Successful consumption of all dots in a level advances the player to the next, more challenging level.

The evaluation in this game begins with a certain number of lives allotted to the player and each contact with ghost results in loss of life. The seemingly routine play is coupled with energizers, warp tunnels, and bonus items. The evaluation ends when the lives count is exhausted.

8.4.1.5 StarCraft (1998)

StarCraft [55] is a military science fiction-based real-time strategy game developed by Blizzard Entertainment. Instead of a single protagonist, the game features three different intelligent races—Terrans, Zerg, and Protoss—each fighting to establish dominance over others. Each species is granted its own unique set of strengths, powers, and abilities. The game ensures that no race has an innate advantage over any other and that there is uniqueness in the composition of each race.

The primary focus of the game is on strengthening the capabilities of the chosen race by collecting resources, building bases, constitute armies, and finally wage wars against the other race. Though each race relay on two key resources, minerals and vespene gas, and supply mechanic operates in the same fashion for each race, the resource management for each race is unique as the nature of the supply differs between the races. On a very similar tone, base constructions for different species all differ and provides different possibilities as well challenges. Given the competitive nature of the game, it has been widely credited with revolutionizing the real-time strategy genre and rightly so, considering the scaling AI that has been used in it.

8.4.2 Popular Datasets

Data is the primary and essential element for research in any domain. In-game content creation, some popular corpora are employed frequently when PCG is integrated with GANs. Hence, in the following subsections, a brief overview of these datasets is mentioned.

8.4.2.1 Video Game Level Corpus (VGLC)

VGLC [56] is the most famous repository used by researchers for accessing data to be used for training purposes in the field of PCG for gameplay. The corpus comprises 12 games that include some of the prominent games in PCG such as *Super Mario Bros*, *The Legend of Zelda*, *DOOM*, and many more. The data has been annotated as Graph, Tiles, and Vectors. Moreover, most of the data is currently being employed in research for arcade level generations.

8.4.2.2 Idgames Archive

Idgames archive [57, 58] is the primary source for Doom engine-related tools, levels, and modifications maintained by the community. This repository has been one of the largest open-source archives for all the Doom data, and although it started in 1994, it still receives weekly entries for *Doom* games that further assists in the research domain. The database consists of several different types of training data for Doom including, levels, textures or skins, music-related, and many more.

8.4.2.3 General Video Game AI (GVG-AI)

General Video Game AI (GVGAI) [59, 60] was initially introduced by researchers by encouraging novel research in the domain of gameplay to generate game agents with unknown testing environments. This competition framework comprises mainly two PCG generation objectives namely, level generation and rule generation. Moreover, recently this platform has been used by researchers as small dataset for different PCG implementations in generating gameplay content.

8.4.2.4 Sarah and Lucy Character

This dataset comprises two characters, Sarah and Lucy [53], selected from Trajes Fatais arcade that is integrated for gameplay character generation or sprite production.

From the Trajes Fatais game, we selected the Sarah and Lucy characters as datasets to evaluate the usefulness of the Pix2Pix architecture. The Sarah character has only 87 completed sprites while 207 uncompleted ones. It's also a character with a relatively fluid personality, with many smooth and complex areas. Lucy, on the other hand, is completed, so it has 530 completely drawn sprites and is relatively simple to draw, with mainly smooth features.

8.4.2.5 NASA SRTM30

The NASA SRTM dataset [61] contains the elevation map data of different regions of the planet. This corpus is used to create a height map using the points from the Shuttle Radar Topography Mission (SRTM) dataset. Moreover, the data comprises of single texture where white depict high values in comparison to black regions depicting low height values.

Apart from the above-mentioned datasets, there were other corpora used as data for producing arcade game content that was manually created by the researchers for their specific purpose. Moreover, of these five training datasets, the Sarah and Lucy characters and NASA SRTM30 have been comparatively less popular among the researchers. Table 8.2 depicts details regarding the three prominent datasets for research.

TABLE 8.2

Popular Datasets in Video Game Content Generation

Dataset	Number of Games Available	Most Prominent Games	Dataset Composition
VGLC [56]	12	*Super Mario Bros, Doom, The Legend of Zelda*	Tiles, Graph, Vector
Idgames Archive [57, 58]	1	*Doom*	Levels, Skins, Music, etc.
GVGAI [59, 60]	No specific count	Random generation of data	Two categories: level and rule generation

8.5 FUTURE ADVANCEMENT

A noteworthy pressing issue commonly encountered in GANs specialized for games is the scarcity of the research done for aspects such as character generation, terrain generation, and texture synthesis for games. While there has been extensive research for level map generation for video games, other functional aspects have hardly seen any exploration. Even cosmetic aspects such as texture generation, vegetation generation, or utilization of different architecture do not have any substantial automation development. Some potential promising architectures for developing GANs for games are cycle consistent adversarial networks, that are capable of translating the styles and characteristics in one sample into another; and conditional GANs, capable of investigating the incorporation of additional constraint checkers into the solver and explore their impact and how the generated content address specific learning objectives. Another possibility for future scope is to explore the self-attention GAN model which can better track patterns with long-range dependencies.

A noticeably rarely researched area is the two-stage GAN framework for games, due to the obvious extensive computational requirements. There have been notable developments in deep generative modeling in recent years. However, none of the models, new or old, has shown to satisfactorily generate content on its own. An obvious step in this regard would be the development of more sophisticated models. Another not-so-obvious yet potentially more practical approach would be to use a mixture of existing models. The Generator and Discriminator both could be based on different models or two sets of GANs could be trained on different models and the final results could be combined to generate more realistic content. This idea opens up a plethora of possibilities in games as this lifts the burden of single-handedly creating rich, believable content from a single GAN. A game-based GAN that can perfectly create 3D meshes can be coupled with another GAN that adds texture to the mesh, resulting in a richer experience. It also holds the possibility to be further developed into a full-fledged tool to aid creators and producers in generating high-quality content. This, of course, comes with its computational limitations, and extensive research is required. Also, more advanced GAN-specific loss reductions need to be explored to ensure minimization of reconstruction losses, especially in height maps and prevent mode collapse and partial mode coverage.

Using GANs for games is essentially optimization of a Minimax objective [5], that is optimizing multiple objectives jointly. Theoretically, this is a Nash equilibrium (NE) problem; but given the NP-hard nature of finding a global NE, gradient-based algorithms, especially gradient descent ascent (GDA), are more commonly used. But this approach too comes at a cost. The GDA has its inherent flaws when dealing with joint optimization. There is a potential for the existence of cycles, and therefore there are no convergence guarantees [62]. Next, in case the gradient descent does converge, there is a high probability that the rate is too slow in practice as recurrent dynamics require extremely small learning rates [62, 63]. The existence of multiple objectives leaves no room for progress monitor [63]. From the game-theoretic aspect, the duality gap (DG) [64] seems to be a natural consequence and can be used to evaluate the performance of GANs. Interestingly the evolution of the DG tracks the convergence of the algorithm to an optimum. Even so, only the issue of progress monitoring, using DG, has been satisfactorily catered to. There has been the utilization of Parallel Nash Memory (PNM) or the addition of fake uniform data to act as a guiding component for adversarial training [10]. Another suggestion has been to optimize games centric GANs by using mixing strategies, such as NE itself with gradient descent. But so far this is only of theoretical interest as there is no known DL (i.e., gradient-based) method yet to optimize these mixed strategies that can stand the large support sizes needed in games.

Yet another unexplored area in game-centric GAN development is disentanglement. Disentanglement is learning to distinguish between distinct, informative factors of variations of data. Unlike Bayesian generative models with their probabilistic framework, in GANs, there is the perpetual absence of sample likelihood and posterior inference for latent variables. Therefore, learning a factorized representation or especially disentangling the interclass variation in GANs poses an obvious obstruction in its advancement. Improvisation in disentanglement for GANs specifically utilized for games is essential to attain the goals of believability and expressivity that PCG demands. There are limited disentanglement methods for GANs and even more scarce in respect to gaming requirements. They can be classified into supervised ones and unsupervised ones, however, the theoretical impossibility of unsupervised disentanglement learning without inductive biases [65] has been a topic of debate and has led to a piqued interest in contrastive learning [66–68], another barely explored area, that needs little supervision, in contrast, to complete unsupervised alternatives.

8.6 CONCLUSION

GANs-based PCG for games has an excitingly promising potential to significantly reduce costs and development time of games, improvise replay values by producing high-quality fresh content with incredible aesthetics, while also managing the optimization of memory. A fairly modern research topic, it is the descendent from ML (DL) based PCG and is yet to be fully explored and the therefore little intersection of academic research and industrial development is found. This survey attempts to provide a comprehensive flow of how constructive PCG paved the path for AI-based PCG and consequently MLPCG and eventually to PCG-GAN. It lists the various challenges faced and potentials of former PCG models—constructive, search-based, solver-based, simple CNN-based, and other regenerative-based models, among others. This chapter also explores how PCG-GAN can prove to be a futuristic attempt at providing a rich, photorealistic gaming experience and provide playable, authentic gaming content superior to prior generated content and comparable to human augmentations-based creations. A multitude of PCG models is examined, each with a detailed description so that this survey can act as a single point stop for a comprehensive overview of all the work done in this field. Since the major point under consideration is to demonstrate the potential of GAN on games, a variety of GAN-based games are presented along with the datasets they utilize. This section also sheds light on some of the ready-to-use off-the-shelf tools that have already been and can further be utilized for advancement. Different models based on which various researchers have trained the GANs for games have also been elaborated on to understand and build upon.

Beyond the typical problem of hardware and GPU-related issues faced in most GAN applications, the specific problems associated with the application of GANs for games, such as the inability for disentanglement, lack of exploration of aspect creations beyond level generations, overpowering of networks, etc. have also been briefly discussed. Based on the problems faced an enormous amount of scope for future work, this chapter concludes with the elucidation of some potential future works that can be carried out for further advancements in the application of GANs for games.

REFERENCES

1. Hendrikx, M., Meijer, S., Velden, J.V.D., & Iosup, A. Procedural Content Generation for Games: A Survey. ACM Transactions on Multimedia Computing, Communications and Applications (ACM TOMCCAP), 9, 1–22 (2013).
2. Barriga, N.A. A Short Introduction to Procedural Content Generation Algorithms for Videogames. International Journal on Artificial Intelligence Tools, 28(11), 1–12 (2019), 1930001.
3. Togelius, J., Yannakakis, G.N., Stanley, K., & Browne, C. Search-Based Procedural Content Generation: A Taxonomy and Survey. IEEE Transactions on Computational Intelligence and AI in Games, 3, 172–186 (2011).
4. Smith, A.M., & Mateas, M. Answer Set Programming for Procedural Content Generation: A Design Space Approach. IEEE Transactions on Computational Intelligence and AI in Games, 3, 187–200 (2011).
5. Goodfellow, I.J., Pouget-Abadie, J., Mirza, M., Xu, B., Warde-Farley, D., Ozair, S., Courville, A.C., & Bengio, Y. Generative Adversarial Nets, NIPS, 2672–2680 (2014).
6. Kingma, D.P., & Welling, M. Auto-Encoding Variational Bayes. CoRR. abs/1312.6114 (2014).
7. Greff, K., Srivastava, R., Koutník, J., Steunebrink, B., & Schmidhuber, J. LSTM: A Search Space Odyssey. IEEE Transactions on Neural Networks and Learning Systems, 28, 2222–2232 (2017).
8. Hochreiter, S., & Schmidhuber, J. LSTM can Solve Hard Long Time Lag Problems. NIPS (1996).
9. Summerville, A., Snodgrass, S., Guzdial, M., Holmgård, C., Hoover, A.K., Isaksen, A., Nealen, A., & Togelius, J. Procedural Content Generation via Machine Learning (PCGML). IEEE Transactions on Games, 10, 257–270 (2018).
10. Oliehoek, F.A., Savani, R., Gallego-Posada, J., Pol, E.V., Jong, E.D., & Groß, R. GANGs: Generative Adversarial Network Games. ArXiv. abs/1712.00679 (2017).
11. Kempka, M., Wydmuch, M., Runc, G., Toczek, J., & Jaśkowski, W. ViZDoom: A Doom-based AI research platform for visual reinforcement learning. 2016 IEEE Conference on Computational Intelligence and Games (CIG), 1–8 (2016).
12. Esparcia-Alcázar, A., García, A.M., Guervós, J.J., & García-Sánchez, P. Controlling bots in a First-Person Shooter game using genetic algorithms. IEEE Congress on Evolutionary Computation, 1–8 (2010).
13. Bojarski, S., & Congdon, C. REALM: A Rule-Based Evolutionary Computation Agent that Learns to Play Mario. Proceedings of the 2010 IEEE Conference on Computational Intelligence and Games, 83–90 (2010).
14. Rhalibi, A., & Merabti, M. A Hybrid Fuzzy ANN System for Agent Adaptation in a First-Person Shooter. International Journal of Computer Games Technology, 2008, 432365:1–432365:18 (2008).
15. Karpov, I.V., Schrum, J., & Miikkulainen, R. Believable Bot Navigation via Playback of Human Traces. Believable Bots (2012).

16. Volz, V., Schrum, J., Liu, J., Lucas, S., Smith, A., & Risi, S. Evolving Mario Levels in the Latent Space of a Deep Convolutional Generative Adversarial Network. Proceedings of the Genetic and Evolutionary Computation Conference (2018).

17. Awiszus, M., Schubert, F., & Rosenhahn, B. TOAD-GAN: Coherent Style Level Generation from a Single Example. Proceedings of the AAAI Conference on Artificial Intelligence and Interactive Digital Entertainment, 16(1), 10–16. ArXiv. abs/2008.01531 (2020).

18. Summerville, A., & Mateas, M. Super Mario as a String: Platformer Level Generation via LSTMs. ArXiv. abs/1603.00930 (2016).

19. Sarkar, A., Yang, Z., & Cooper, S. Controllable Level Blending between Games using Variational Autoencoders. ArXiv. abs/2002.11869 (2020).

20. Kim, S.W., Zhou, Y., Philion, J., Torralba, A., & Fidler, S. Learning to Simulate Dynamic Environments With GameGAN. 2020 IEEE/CVF Conference on Computer Vision and Pattern Recognition (CVPR), 1228–1237 (2020).

21. Dahlskog, S., Togelius, J., & Nelson, M.J. Linear Levels Through n-Grams. MindTrek, 200–206 (2014).

22. Jain, R., Isaksen, A., Holmgard, C., & Togelius, J. Autoencoders for level generation, repair, and recognition. In Proceedings of the ICCC Workshop on Computational Creativity and Games (2016).

23. Snodgrass, S., & Ontañón, S. Experiments in Map Generation Using Markov Chains. FDG (2014).

24. Summerville, A., & Mateas, M. Sampling Hyrule: Multi-Technique Probabilistic Level Generation for Action Role Playing Games. AIIDE (2015).

25. Lee, S., Isaksen, A., Holmgård, C., & Togelius, J. Predicting Resource Locations in Game Maps Using Deep Convolutional Neural Networks. AAAI (2016).

26. Liu, J., Snodgrass, S., Khalifa, A., Risi, S., Yannakakis, G.N., & Togelius, J. Deep Learning for Procedural Content Generation. Neural Computing and Applications. 33, 19–37 (2021).

27. Giacomello, E., Lanzi, P.L., & Loiacono, D. DOOM Level Generation Using Generative Adversarial Networks. 2018 IEEE Games, Entertainment, Media Conference (GEM), 316–323 (2018).

28. Doom (franchise). This page was last edited on 13 September 2021, at 01:55 (UTC) https://en.wikipedia.org/wiki/Doom (franchise).

29. Super Mario Bros. This page was last edited on 13 September 2021, at 17:08 (UTC) https://en.wikipedia.org/wiki/Super_Mario_Bros.

30. Hansen, N., Müller, S., & Koumoutsakos, P. Reducing the Time Complexity of the Derandomized Evolution Strategy with Covariance Matrix Adaptation (CMA-ES). Evolutionary Computation, 11, 1–18 (2003).

31. Giacomello, E., Lanzi, P.L., & Loiacono, D. Searching the Latent Space of a Generative Adversarial Network to Generate DOOM Levels. 2019 IEEE Conference on Games (CoG), 1–8 (2019).

32. Park, K., Mott, B., Min, W., Boyer, K., Wiebe, E., & Lester, J.C. Generating Educational Game Levels with Multistep Deep Convolutional Generative Adversarial Networks. 2019 IEEE Conference on Games (CoG), 1–8 (2019).

33. Torrado, R., Khalifa, A., Green, M.C., Justesen, N., Risi, S., & Togelius, J. Bootstrapping Conditional GANs for Video Game Level Generation. 2020 IEEE Conference on Games (CoG), 41–48 (2020).

34. Zhang, H., Goodfellow, I.J., Metaxas, D.N., & Odena, A. Self-Attention Generative Adversarial Networks. ICML (2019).

35. Gutierrez, J., & Schrum, J. Generative Adversarial Network Rooms in Generative Graph Grammar Dungeons for The Legend of Zelda. 2020 IEEE Congress on Evolutionary Computation (CEC), 1–8 (2020).

36. The Legend of Zelda. This page was last edited on 12 September 2021, at 15:53 (UTC) https://en.wikipedia.org/wiki/The_Legend_of_Zelda.
37. Schrum, J., Volz, V., & Risi, S. CPPN2GAN: Combining Compositional Pattern Producing Networks and GANs for Large-Scale Pattern Generation. Proceedings of the 2020 Genetic and Evolutionary Computation Conference (2020).
38. Stanley, K. Compositional Pattern Producing Networks: A Novel Abstraction of Development. Genetic Programming and Evolvable Machines, 8, 131–162 (2007).
39. Shaham, T.R., Dekel, T., & Michaeli, T. SinGAN: Learning a Generative Model From a Single Natural Image. 2019 IEEE/CVF International Conference on Computer Vision (ICCV), 4569–4579 (2019).
40. Bontrager, P., & Togelius, J. Fully Differentiable Procedural Content Generation through Generative Playing Networks. ArXiv. abs/2002.05259 (2020).
41. Gobbi, J., Liello, L.D., Ardino, P., Morettin, P., Teso, S., & Passerini, A. Efficient Generation of Structured Objects with Constrained Adversarial Networks. ArXiv. abs/2007.13197 (2020).
42. Irfan, A., Zafar, A., & Hassan, S. Evolving Levels for General Games Using Deep Convolutional Generative Adversarial Networks. 2019 11th Computer Science and Electronic Engineering (CEEC), 96–101 (2019).
43. Kumaran, V., Mott, B., & Lester, J.C. Generating Game Levels for Multiple Distinct Games With a Common Latent Space. AAAI, 16(1), 109–115 (2020).
44. Beckham, C., & Pal, C. A Step Towards Procedural Terrain Generation With GANs. ArXiv. abs/1707.03383 (2017).
45. Wulff-Jensen, A., Rant, N.N., Møller, T.N., & Billeskov, J. Deep Convolutional Generative Adversarial Network for Procedural 3D Landscape Generation Based on DEM. ArtsIT/DLI, 85–94 (2017).
46. Ferranti, Jonathan de. Viewfinder Panoramas (2012).
47. Spick, R.R., & Walker, J. Realistic and Textured Terrain Generation using GANs. European Conference on Visual Media Production (2019).
48. Jetchev, N., Bergmann, U., & Vollgraf, R. Texture Synthesis With Spatial Generative Adversarial Networks. ArXiv. abs/1611.08207 (2016).
49. Wang, T., & Kurabayashi, S. Sketch2Map: A Game Map Design Support System Allowing Quick Hand Sketch Prototyping. 2020 IEEE Conference on Games (CoG), 596–599 (2020).
50. Fadaeddini, A., Majidi, B., & Eshghi, M. A Case Study of Generative Adversarial Networks for Procedural Synthesis of Original Textures in Video Games. 2018 2nd National and 1st International Digital Games Research Conference: Trends, Technologies, and Applications (DGRC), 118–122 (2018).
51. Horsley, L., & Liebana, D.P. Building an Automatic Sprite Generator with Deep Convolutional Generative Adversarial Networks. 2017 IEEE Conference on Computational Intelligence and Games (CIG), 134–141 (2017).
52. Hong, S., Kim, S., & Kang, S. Game Sprite Generator Using a Multi Discriminator GAN. KSII Transactions on Internet and Information Systems, 13, 4255–4269 (2019).
53. Serpa, Y.R., & Rodrigues, M.A. Towards Machine-Learning Assisted Asset Generation for Games: A Study on Pixel Art Sprite Sheets. 2019 18th Brazilian Symposium on Computer Games and Digital Entertainment (SBGames), 182–191 (2019).
54. Pac-Man. This page was last edited on 14 September 2021, at 00:21 (UTC) https://en.wikipedia.org/wiki/Pac-Man.
55. Blizzard Entertainment. StarCraft (1998). https://starcraft2.com/en-us/.
56. Summerville, A., Snodgrass, S., Mateas, M., & Ontañón, S. The VGLC: The Video Game Level Corpus. ArXiv. abs/1606.07487 (2016).
57. https://www.doomworld.com/idgames/.
58. idgames archive | Doom Wiki | Fandom, https://doom.fandom.com/wiki/Idgames_archive.

59. http://www.gvgai.net/.
60. Khalifa, A., Liebana, D.P., Lucas, S., & Togelius, J. General Video Game Level Generation. Proceedings of the Genetic and Evolutionary Computation Conference 2016 (2016).
61. https://topex.ucsd.edu/WWW_html/srtm30_plus.html.
62. Mescheder, L.M., Geiger, A., & Nowozin, S. Which Training Methods for GANs do actually Converge? ICML (2018).
63. Gidel, G., Hemmat, R.A., Pezeshki, M., Huang, G., Priol, R.L., Lacoste-Julien, S., & Mitliagkas, I. Negative Momentum for Improved Game Dynamics. ArXiv. abs/1807.04740 (2019).
64. Chen, X., Duan, Y., Houthooft, R., Schulman, J., Sutskever, I., & Abbeel, P. InfoGAN: Interpretable Representation Learning by Information Maximizing Generative Adversarial Nets. NIPS (2016).
65. Locatello, F., Bauer, S., Lucic, M., Gelly, S., Schölkopf, B., & Bachem, O. Challenging Common Assumptions in the Unsupervised Learning of Disentangled Representations. ArXiv. abs/1811.12359 (2019).
66. He, K., Fan, H., Wu, Y., Xie, S., & Girshick, R.B. Momentum Contrast for Unsupervised Visual Representation Learning. 2020 IEEE/CVF Conference on Computer Vision and Pattern Recognition (CVPR), 9726–9735 (2020).
67. Wu, Z., Xiong, Y., Yu, S., & Lin, D. Unsupervised Feature Learning via Non-parametric Instance Discrimination. 2018 IEEE/CVF Conference on Computer Vision and Pattern Recognition, 3733–3742 (2018).
68. Chen, T., Kornblith, S., Norouzi, M., & Hinton, G.E. A Simple Framework for Contrastive Learning of Visual Representations. ArXiv. abs/2002.05709 (2020).

Index

A

Adventure Games and Puzzle Design
37, 44
AI for Adaptive Computer Games 37, 41
AI for Computer Games 37, 38
AI in Gaming 37, 60
AI in Video Games: Toward a Unified
Framework 37, 41
AI Latest Techniques in Animation 19, 23
AR Technology 19, 26
VR Technology 19, 28
AI Latest Techniques in Animation
19, 23
AI Reinvent 103, 106
AI'S Role in Animation 19, 21
How AI Replaces Animation 19, 21
Various Agents in AI 19, 22
Alpha-Beta Pruning 8
Augmented Reality 110

C

CBGIR 91, 94
CGANs 127
Classification 65, 81
Complex Game AI 103, 115
Cyclical GANs 128

D

Deep Learning 75, 82, 93
Deep Learning in PCG 137, 142
Deformable Gans for Pose-Based Human Image
Generation 123, 130
Deterministic 104
Diverse Image Generation via Self-Conditioned
GANs 123, 129

E

Early Game 103, 115
eHealth 65, 74
Extended Reality 103, 110

F

Finite State Machines 103, 116
Future Aspects of Animation with AI
19, 33
Futuristic Approach 37

G

Game Theory 3, 6
Gaming Experience 103, 107
Generative Adversarial Networks 123, 126

H

Heuristic Function 3, 4, 5
Home Automation 65, 74
Horror Genre and Video Games 37, 45
Hybrid Fuzzy ANN Systems 139

I

The Image Classification Theory 91, 96
Image Generation and Recognition 123, 127
Image Processing Using Deep Learning 91, 98
Important Architectures in Deep Learning
91, 94
Interactive Narrative 37, 44
Internet of Things (IoT) 65, 67
Communication Block 65, 68
Protocols 65, 69
Sensing Block 65, 68
IoT and 5G Technology 65, 78
IoT Networks 83

L

Logistics 65, 75

M

Machine Learning 91, 92
Minimax Approach 4, 8
MINIMAX Vs APLHA-BETA PRUNING 8
Motionscan Technology 65, 77
MQTT 69, 70
Multi-Discriminator GAN (MDGAN) 146

N

Narrative Game Mechanics 37, 43
Narrative in Video Games 37, 42
Nondeterministic 105

P

PCGML 137, 141
Player Experience 37, 48
Procedural Content Generation (PCG)
137, 140

Q

Q-Algorithm for AI in Gaming 37,
　　60

R

Regression 65, 81

S

SAGANs 128
Search Tree 2, 3, 8
Simulation Based on Physics 103, 108
Smart Agriculture 65, 74
Stack GANs 128
Supervised Learning 65, 80
Systematic Analysis of Image Generation Using
　　GANs 123, 131

T

Three-Dimensional Visualization Techniques
　　103, 108
TOAD-GANs 139
The Traditional and Modern Animation
　　19, 30

U

Utility and Application 14, 15

V

Virtual Reality 103, 109
Voice in Gaming 103, 107

Z

Zero-Sum Game 4, 6